**Peace! Books! Freedom!
The Secret History of
a Radical London Building**

# CONTENTS

**We need books,
we need peace,
and we need them right here,
in the heart of King's Cross,
Diana Shelley**

# INTRODUCTION

In 1959, 5 Caledonian Road, a narrow, terraced building around the corner from King's Cross station in London, became the home of the pacifist newspaper *Peace News* and Housmans bookshop. Officially called 'Peace House' but more commonly known as 'the *Peace News* building', Housmans or simply 5 Cally Road, the building remains, more than sixty years later, a radical oasis in central London.

Housmans, now one of the oldest radical bookshops in the country, is on the ground floor and basement. Climb the steep stairs above the bookshop and you find four floors of small rooms used by community and campaign groups as offices. Over the years more than 50 radical and progressive groups have been based in the building.

Using oral histories recorded with some of the people who have been involved with the building, this book aims to explore the significance of 5 Cally Road and how it has continued as a radical centre for such an extended period.

At first, the building was envisioned as a peace 'movement centre' that first and foremost provided space for *Peace News* to be written, packed and distributed. Housmans was seen partly as a fundraising venture to support *Peace News*, although it did also publish and distribute peace movement literature. However, this changed between 1974 and 1994 when *Peace News* moved out of 5 Cally Road. With the newspaper gone, Housmans became more independent and in the 1980s developed its own, separate identity as a radical bookshop. From the 1970s onwards the building was increasingly used by a diverse range of groups, not only those explicitly concerned with nonviolence, peace and anti-militarism but also LGBTQ+ organisations, environmental and animal rights, community and campaigning groups.

The building has weathered many kinds of attacks: it has been the scene of bombings, arrests, police raids and espionage. Since the 1960s, there have also been several plans to redevelop the area, which would have led to the building's demolition. That it remains is thanks to the trustees' refusal to sell it and the campaigning and lobbying of the local community.

It has been a safe space to meet and work for many groups that may not have found a sympathetic home elsewhere. Inside, those campaigning around unpopular causes could feel secure, as one interviewee, Lesley Mair, explained to us, 'you knew that once you got in that door, however wacky people might have thought your views were, this was a place where you would find support.'

Julian Hows, who was part of the Gay Liberation Front and later London Gay Switchboard, which was based in the building from 1974 until 1993, reflected that 5 Cally Road:

> gave [Switchboard] a space where probably no one else would. Simple as that, you know? And the space for people to come together to organise around a common activity, cannot be undervalued. ... it created an umbrella, under which we could take shade.

Housmans bookshop remains a place anyone can walk into and access progressive, radical ideas. As Ramsey Kanaan, anarchist publisher and distributor, told us:

> No one comes with their politics fully formed … For anyone and everyone that is a process. For that process to even happen there has to be a literal and physical way of entering that process. So, the main importance of Housmans is it actually exists as a physical space, and hence, not just figuratively, but literally, Housmans remains an entryway and a gateway to a whole world of radical ideas, radical histories, radical potentialities.

Mike Jackson, co-founder of Lesbians and Gays Support the Miners, pointed out that the left has 'lost enormous ground' since Thatcher was elected in 1979, which makes the building 'much more important than it's ever been … because it's one of the last outposts.' As Ippy D, a former editor of *Peace News*, observed, having a physical space from which to organise is often crucial:

> It's only when you actually have a physical space, and that can be a small piece of land, it can be a peace camp, it could be 5 Cally Road, it doesn't matter what it is, but if you have a space and you can hold that space, then you can make things happen. If you don't have any space … it's actually very difficult to organise things, to create strong movements.

This book is based on the archive collected by the history project, 5 Cally Road, which ran between 2020 and 2022. This work was made possible by funding from the National Lottery Heritage Fund. From 2020 to 2021, with a team of talented and dedicated people aged between 18 and 25, we collected documents, photographs and thirty-four oral history interviews for a 5 Cally Road archive which is housed at the Bishopsgate Institute. The project told the story of the building and some of the movements it has been connected to over the years. Working with theatre director Lucy Allen and other creative professionals the project's volunteers made radio plays, animated monologues, music videos and poetry inspired by the building. With sound artist Wajid Yaseen they made a sound installation for Housmans bookshop in 2021. You can explore the project's archive and creative work at 5callyroad.org

All of the oral history interviews quoted in this book are from the 5 Cally Road archive, with the exception of the interview with Harry Mister, who was interviewed by Alan Dein in 2005 for the King's Cross Voices oral history project. The 5 Cally Road interviews were conducted remotely during the COVID-19 pandemic.

Many people have kept the building going over the years by attending board meetings, organising repairs and raising money. We only tell a fraction of their stories here. Some groups and individuals have had more attention paid to them than others, other significant people and organisations are missing entirely. The way the accounts have been selected is not meant to imply that the perspectives of any of the people featured are more important than those of others not quoted. For reasons of space and focus, some of the fascinating interviews we recorded have not been included in this book, and there are many stories in the archive we have collected that deal with subjects less relevant to the building that go untold here. All the interviews we recorded can be explored in full at Bishopsgate Institute in London, where they are archived.

This book is not meant to provide in-depth analysis of any of the groups, campaigns or movements that feature in it. It does not engage in debates around their tactics or ideas, unless they have impacted directly on events within the building. However, the people we recorded often disagreed with each other and some critiqued their earlier selves for opinions they once held. Through the diversity of these recorded perspectives, we catch glimpses of the evolution of ideas and practices over time.

The structure follows a rough chronology, so that we can see how wider changes develop and affect what happens within the building. At intervals the chronology breaks to consider a particular group or campaign in detail, where the events related need to be told in sequence.

CHAPTER 1, A Movement Centre, sets the scene for the building's opening, during the busiest years of the nuclear disarmament movement, starting with the 1958 Aldermaston march (the year before the building opened) through to 1963.

CHAPTER 2, Revolutionary Projects, looks at the period between 1963 and 1974, describing how *Peace News*, and by extension 5 Cally Road, had to find a way forward as the wider political context shifted and a younger generation with new ideas got involved. This chapter ends with *Peace News* leaving 5 Cally Road, and London, for a new start in Nottingham.

CHAPTER 3, Jolly Good Tenants, is dedicated to the Gay Liberation Front, who had an office in the building between 1971 and 1974.

CHAPTER 4, Not So Peaceful in King's Cross looks at the turbulent years between 1974 and 1979, when the building was bombed twice, harboured an escaped fugitive, was raided by police and involved in three political trials.

CHAPTER 5, Keeping the Lights On, is about Switchboard (previously London Gay Switchboard) who ran their 24-hour helpline in 5 Cally Road from 1974 until 1993.

CHAPTER 6, Anarchy, Peace and Freedom, looks at the building from 1979 to 1987. Most of this chapter is given over to Housmans in the early to mid-1980s, covering its connection with the anarcho-punk scene, the transition to the bookshop being run by a collective of its workers and debates around what being a 'movement bookshop' might mean.

CHAPTER 7, Incurable Optimism, looks at the building from 1987 until the mid-1990s, when a scheme to build a rail link to the Channel Tunnel in King's Cross threatened to demolish the whole neighbourhood, including 5 Cally Road, and Housmans entered a long financial crisis. London Greenpeace, who had an office in the building, was embroiled in England's longest ever trial when two of its members were sued for libel by McDonald's and was spied on by both undercover police and corporate agents.

CHAPTER 8, Sense of Permanence, opens in 1994, when *Peace News* came back to the building along with anti-militarist organisation War Resisters' International. Another development threatened 5 Cally Road's future around the turn of the century, but once that danger had been successfully fought off by the local community, the building was renovated, and the bookshop began to pull itself out of its financial trouble. From 2007 the bookshop was revitalised and is now arguably doing better than at any other time in its long history.

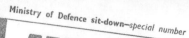

# PEACE NEWS

## FOR NON-VIOLENCE AND UNILATERAL DISARMAMENT

No. 1,287

London, February 24, 1961

SIXPENCE    US Air Express
Edition 10 India

# TRIUMPH OF 100   FOR COMMITTEE

LAST Saturday's sit-down outside the Ministry of Defence in London was joined by about 4,000 people, apart from several thousand supporters who added their solidarity.

This act of mass civil disobedience, organised by the Committee of 100, demanded " the complete rejection by our country of nuclear weapons and all policies and alliances that depend upon them." It was aimed especially at the Polaris agreement with the USA.

The Committee's declaration—which was posted on the Ministry's door, and is on page five of Peace News—concluded: " Our action today is the first step in a campaign of non-violent civil disobedience. We hereby serve notice

### INSIDE

### BERTRAND RUSSELL

explains why Britain should get out of NATO and adopt a policy of neutralism

page nine

### PAGES OF PICTURES

of last Saturday's sit-down in London outside the Ministry of Defence

pages five-eight

## MASS RESISTANC

### SATURDAY DECEMBER 9

Wethersfield
Ruislip
Brize Norton
York
Manchester
Bristol
Cardiff

Committee of 100

13 C

# Peace

# The spies we

On Thursday, April 11, a pamphlet entitled " Danger Official Secret RSG 6" was circulated to the national press, political parties, prominent personalities in the peace movement including Bertrand Russell, Albert Schweitzer and

# CHAPTER 1

# A MOVEMENT CENTRE

## Aldermaston

When 5 Cally Road opened in 1959 as a home for *Peace News* and Housmans bookshop, *Peace News* was already two decades old. It began printing in 1936 as a weekly newspaper, aiming to serve 'all who work for peace'. Housmans had first opened in 1945 in Shaftesbury Avenue, central London. Both were projects of the pacifist Peace Pledge Union (PPU), and the bookshop was inspired by PPU sponsor, writer, illustrator and activist Laurence Housman, who also campaigned for women's suffrage and gay rights.[1]

Housmans closed as a physical shop in 1948, but Harry Mister, who would later be the driving force behind 5 Cally Road, carried it on as a mail order business from the *Peace News* offices. Before 5 Cally Road opened, *Peace News* and Housmans shared crowded rented offices above a shop in Finsbury Park, north London.

The Aldermaston march in 1958 inspired those involved to find a more sustainable home. In 1958, the *Peace News* office was also being used by the newly formed Direct Action Committee Against Nuclear War (DAC), an informal group of individuals with a shared background in pacifism. The DAC were organising a four-day march from London to the atomic weapons establishment at Aldermaston, and the idea had caught on in a big way. Michael Randle, an active member, remembered the months in the run-up to Easter 1958 as exciting and a little overwhelming:

> It was quite worrying in a sense because it took off in such a big way. Whereas we had [previously] organised on quite a small scale, suddenly there were people volunteering from all over the place and setting up groups to try and further this ... And the people working for *Peace News* were getting quite impatient, they could never get on the [phone] line, because it was always blocked by the enquiries about Aldermaston. So, [the editor] Hugh Brock had to arrange for a separate phone line to be installed so that *Peace News* would be able to use their own phone line.

An artist called Gerald Holtom got in touch, offering to design a symbol for the march, as Michael Randle explained:

> He came up to the *Peace News* office in Finsbury Park and produced a set of sketches, which he explained as the symbol representing the semaphore signal for N and D and drew a circle round it. And that is now the famous nuclear disarmament symbol. ... It was an odd symbol to begin with, but ... once we started producing our leaflets, it caught on like wildfire.[2]

---

1  In 1907, Laurence Housman co-founded the Men's League for Women's Suffrage. He was also a member of the Order of Chaeronea, a secret society for homosexual men, and in 1913, with Edward Carpenter and others, he founded the British Society for the Study of Sex Psychology, which aimed to combat legal discrimination against homosexuality.

2  American civil rights activist Bayard Rustin spoke in Trafalgar Square at the beginning of the march. He took the new symbol back to the States with him, where it became known as the peace symbol.

HOUSMANS BOOKSHOP :: OPENING CEREMONY :: 26TH OCTOBER 1945

HOWARD WHITTEN :: HUGH I'ANSON FAUSSET :: PATRICK FIGGIS :: LLEWELLYN KIER :: TREFOR KENDALL DAVIES :: DORIS REGIS :: HARRY MISTER
EILEEN AGER :: :: LAURENCE HOUSMAN :: GEOFFREY GILBERT :: HENRY RUTLAND :: IRENE BARCLAY :: DUNCAN CHRISTIE :: JOHN BARCLAY

Many people and organisations contributed to organising the march: the New Left's Partisan Coffee House in Soho helped distribute publicity, jazz musicians volunteered to play along the route, film-makers got together to record the day and the London Co-operative Society made sandwiches and hot drinks to keep the marchers going. Offers of accommodation for the marchers poured in from churches, Quaker meeting houses and people who lived along the route.

Several thousand people made the march from London to Aldermaston in 1958. The event marked the beginning of a broad-based campaign for nuclear disarmament.

TOP: Housmans bookshop opening ceremony on 26 October 1945 at 124 Shaftsbury Avenue. Laurence Housman is fifth from the left, Harry Mister on the far right

BOTTOM: Aldermaston march to London, 1963

Aldermaston march to London, 1963

## The Building Opens

Exciting as it was, the experience of organising the march while running a paper had 'stretched the [*Peace News*] offices far beyond breaking point', as Harry Mister later wrote.[3] Luckily, *Peace News* received a timely letter from a young curate from East Yorkshire, Tom Willis, who had recently inherited a large sum of money from a relative. Set to become a priest working in deprived areas, he wanted to give his inheritance away to a pacifist group. (He had developed pacifist beliefs during his period of National Service in the army.)

For several years, Harry Mister, who worked as the manager of *Peace News* and Housmans bookshop, had been trying to set up a 'movement centre'.[4] Tom Willis's offer came at the perfect time. As Harry Mister explained, when interviewed in 2005, he jumped at the chance:

> I had been yearning for years to get to central London and get a proper bookshop going, so I gave him a very full set up of starting a Peace Centre near Central London and getting offices for our organizations and the bookshop ... in the end he coughed up £5,000, a vast amount in those days and I went hunting for premises and found this shop in the Cally Road which again cost us about £5,000.[5]

The donation was supposed to remain anonymous, but news leaked out. Tom Willis's family found out and were not pleased to hear he'd given his inheritance away to pacifists. Ann Willis, who married him after the donation had been made, remembers her mother joking 'at least you went where money had been.'

The building was narrow and terraced but was extended in the back, giving plenty of space to work in. Nearly 100 years old, it had been a post office in Victorian times. Its most recent occupants were a catering company, which had left equipment and a refrigerator room in the basement. It needed renovating and young volunteers from the Pacifist Youth Action Group were enlisted to help. Harry Mister recalled:

> We had a marvellous new action group on Blackstock Road who then moved in and literally lived at Cally Road for three months and they did all the donkey work of converting the place. We had so many marvellous workers, an architect who designed Letchworth Garden City came and did the architectural work for us.[6]

One of these workers was Ian Dixon, who had recently hitchhiked to India to learn about the Gandhian movement. He was still 'conditioned to wearing leather

3   Harry Mister, 'Housmans Bookshop — A Report', 1972, University of Bradford Special Collections, Archives of *Peace News* Cwl/PN/3/8.

4   Mister, 'Housmans Bookshop — A Report'.

5   Interview with Harry Mister by Alan Dein for King's Cross Voices, 2005, Camden Local Studies and Archives Centre.

6   'Interview with Harry Mister by Alan Dein for King's Cross Voices'.

... sandals. I couldn't wear shoes. And I couldn't begin to think of fitting into a conventional job.'

Instead, he got to work clearing the basement of 5 Cally Road, where he could happily remain in his sandals. He remembered feeling:

really astonished that somebody had given us a building, I mean, I could hardly believe that ... And it meant we could rent out the rooms we didn't need to use, get an income, and cross-subsidise our projects, *Peace News* and Housmans. And that's the way it operated for years.

On 21 November 1959 Housmans Bookshop and 'the new *Peace News* premises in King's Cross, London' were officially opened. Dora Dawtry, the volunteer bookshop manager, turned the key for the cameras. She was watched by Harry Mister, veteran pacifist Sybil Morrison, *Peace News* editor Hugh Brock, its chair Vera Brittain and Tom Willis, there to witness what his money had bought.[7]

'Peace News' was written in large letters across the centre of the building, while on the ground floor, the Housmans shopfront invited people to enter. Inside, each room was named after a recently deceased pacifist (all white men): George Lansbury, Reginald Reynold, Alexander Wilson, Runham Brown, Corder Catchpool, Alfred Salter, Max Plowman, EE Briscoe, Dick Sheppard, Reverend Henry Carter, Alex Wood.[8] The families of the rooms' namesakes were invited to sponsor the rooms to help raise money for renovations. Some of the name plaques still can be found above doors or hidden behind bookshelves in the building.

They saw King's Cross as an ideal location for the new centre, close to the major railway station and central London. The local area was thriving, as Harry Mister recalled:

[It was] a very successful retailing area. On the corner there was a tailor's, around the corner one of London's biggest jewellers, [there was] a Joe Lyons [tea shop], [it was] a very busy shopping area, very near for getting supplies off by rail all over the country and it was a very central area for people who wanted to come and see us. We were very lucky.[9]

There were sympathetic organisations close by. The Movement for Colonial Freedom and the Independent Labour Party also had offices in King's Cross, while the Quaker Friend's House and the Peace Pledge Union were just down the road in Euston.

According to Harry Mister, in its early years, 5 Cally Road was used mostly to write, administer and distribute *Peace News*:

7   *Peace News*, 4 December 1959, 1223 edition.
8   Lady Clare Annesley, 'New Premises for *Peace News* — and a New Centre in London for All Who Work for Peace', University of Bradford Special Collections, Archives of *Peace News* Cwl/PN/5/2.

9   'Interview with Harry Mister by Alan Dein for King's Cross Voices'.
10  'Interview with Harry Mister by Alan Dein for King's Cross Voices'.

*PEACE NEWS*

1223 Dec. 4, 1959 6d. US Air Express Edition 10 cents

17 GOING W
ALL SET F
FINAL PREPARATIONS WERE BE
PROTESTS TEAM'S START TO-
FRENCH ATOM BOMB TESTING

LEFT: Photograph of the opening of 5 Caledonian Road on 21 November 1959. Front row (from left) Hugh Brock, Myrtle Solomon, Sue Mister, unknown, Val Mister, Vera Brittain, Dora Dawtry, unknown, George Plume, Reverend Tom Willis, Stuart Morris Second row: Roy Fry (Pacifist Youth Action Group), Ian Dixon (third from left), Ivy Mister (second from right). Back: Sybil Morrison (left) Harry Mister (centre)

Dora Dawtry, bookshop manager, turns the key at the opening of Housmans Bookshop, which forms part of the new Peace News premises at King's Cross, London. With her left to right are: Arthur Goss, the Rev. Tom Willis (whose gift of £5,700 made the purchase of the building possible), Frank Dawtry, Harry Mister, Vera Brittain, Hugh Brock, Sybil Morrison and Stuart Morris.

RIGHT: Article from *Peace News*, published on 4 December 1959 reporting on the opening of 5 Cally Road on 21 November 1959

First of all, Housmans was only the front bit of the ground floor. We took on the stationery side in a much bigger way and general books for the local community. We have always had a strong feeling of rapport with the local business[es] and residential communities. The rest of the ground floor was used for the distribution work for *Peace News* and as a reception. The offices were upstairs. *Peace News* used all of the first floor and part of the second floor. We had a pacifist publishing firm in a room on the second floor and a charming old couple living on the top floor who looked after the building. In the basement, the back end had the original offices for London CND, which was a hive of activity, stacked us up with people all day. In the middle we had a very big dispatch layout and archive room for *Peace News*. The front end of the basement was the storeroom for our publications and stationery.[10]

Although *Peace News* took up most of the building's space, Housmans quickly developed in its new home into both a peace movement bookshop and a commercial project, as Harry Mister explained:

The bookshop was an interesting compromise because we had to make it viable so we set out to serve the local community and that was rewarding, and enjoyable and local office workers would come in during lunch hours. But we still worked hard on the movement side by doing all these conference bookstalls. We were the agents in Britain for Gandhi's publishing house in India and we distributed all his books to trade in this country. We put a specialist peace display bookshop down in the basement, so it was easier for us to furnish these outside bookstores. We sold a lot of relevant stuff. We were very early

# Christmas Cards
## Books and Gifts for 1959

### LIST AND ORDER FORM

★ Original and lovely Christmas Greetings Cards that convey the true spirit of the season. Large and widely varied range from 2d. to 9d. each.

★ Tasteful and inexpensive Gifts for everyone.

★ Christmas Gift Dressings and Stationery.

★ Peace Diary and Friendship Calendar.

★ Book Gifts selected for all ages.

★ Fund-raising Discounts for Bazaars and orders over £1.

All proceeds from your purchases off this list are devoted to the work of PEACE NEWS for peace and world goodwill.

LEFT: Front cover of a brochure for Christmas cards and books published by Endsleigh Cards and Housmans in 1959, the year 5 Cally Road opened

selling books for pioneers of the environmental movement, we specialised in ecology, and we worked closely with Movement for Colonial Freedom, doing bookstalls with them and keeping their books. It wasn't just a pacifist bookshop, it was a bookshop for all the issues that pertained to developing a peaceful and just, libertarian society.'[11]

To keep *Peace News* going, they needed to raise money to cover its costs. Harry Mister helped; he described himself as 'a repressed entrepreneur, a capitalist who couldn't bear to be it.'[12] Another money-making venture he was involved in was Endsleigh Cards, which was one of the first companies to provide Christmas cards for charities like Oxfam and Barnardo's to sell. By 1962 they were printing three million cards a year. Harry Mister explained:

We ran *Peace News* for many years for on the profits of Endsleigh Cards. They weren't all propaganda but there was always a good section of anti-racist and anti-war illustrations and quotations in them. They were all Christmas cards. My kids, bless them,

11  Interview with Harry Mister by Alan Dein for King's Cross Voices.

12  'Interview with Harry Mister by Alan Dein for Kings Cross Voices'.

13  'Interview with Harry Mister by Alan Dein for Kings Cross Voices.

RIGHT: All Nations at the Crib, Christmas card produced by Endsleigh cards

used to pack thousands of them in cellophane bags to send to Oxfam to sell. I still have a few tucked away.[13]

The *Housmans Peace Diary* was another fundraising venture. First published in 1953 it continues to be produced today and includes a World Peace Directory, listing peace movement organisations and groups around the world.

The *Peace News* Christmas Fair also brought in funds, as Harry Mister described:
That was a very effective rallying of lots of peace people and we would have it at places like Kingsway Hall and Westminster Central Hall and good venues in London. That helped *Peace News* make quite a bit of money. It was also a social event, start in the morning, have lots of stalls and voluntary workers running different stalls and a big outlet for Housmans ... and have a distinguished pacifist to open it in the afternoon. In the evenings we finished up with a concert, an all-day event. Great fun organising. We had so many good voluntary helpers, amazing. I could take things in my stride. I never wanted *Peace News* to be a wholly charity provided organisation, I always wanted it to pay its way.[14]

## Direct Action Committee

While the new building was being established, the nuclear disarmament movement had been developing. The Direct Action Committee (DAC) had their own offices in Finsbury Park but remained connected to *Peace News*. The two organisations shared some of the same key personnel, including the paper's editor, Hugh Brock. It was an optimistic time. *Peace News* wrote in their annual report: 'How shall we sum up 1958? Perhaps as the year in which pacifist-led activities made a great impact on public opinion in Britain and the U.S.A.'[15]

Campaign for Nuclear Disarmament (CND) started just before the Aldermaston march in 1958 and set about building a national campaign. CND hoped to achieve disarmament through Parliament, specifically by persuading the Labour Party to back their cause. After 1958 CND took over the organising of the Aldermaston march, turning it around so it went from Aldermaston to London, putting symbolic pressure on Parliament, rather than the locations where nuclear weapons were produced.

The Direct Action Committee took a different approach and focused on using civil disobedience to protest and disrupt the production of nuclear weapons. They

14    'Interview with Harry Mister by Alan Dein for King's Cross Voices'.

15    '*Peace News* Annual Report 1958–59', University of

Bradford Special Collections, Archives of *Peace News* Cwl/PN/2.

# EASTER MARCH TO
## ALDERMASTON

The Direct Action Committee against Nuclear War invites you to join in
a FOUR DAY FIFTY MILE EASTER MARCH to the Aldermaston Atomic Weapons
Research Establishment as a protest against the production of nuclear
weapons.

The route and schedule for the march will be as follows:-

Good Friday - marchers will assemble at 11 a.m. in Trafalgar Square,
where there will be a short act of repentance for suffering caused in
the past by our dropping and testing of nuclear bombs and dedication
to the struggle against further production of atomic and hydrogen
weapons.  Philip Toynbee, Harold and Sheila Steele and Frank Allaun M.P.
will be on the plinth.  Setting off from Trafalgar Square at 11.30, a
march of about ten miles, with breaks for lunch and tea, should bring us
to Hounslow by 7 p.m., where we shall hold an evening rally.

Saturday - re-assemble at Bell Corner, Hounslow Broadway at 10 a.m.,
and march through Colnbrook and Slough, reaching Maidenhead by the early
evening, where another rally will be held.

Easter Sunday - the assembly point will be Maidenhead station yard.
Marchers will set off at 10 a.m. and march via Knowl Hill to Reading
for a further evening meeting.

Bank Holiday Monday - re-assemble at St. Mary's Butts at 9.50 a.m.
and march on to Aldermaston for a final rally and demonstration.

It is hoped to arrange for tea to be supplied at stopping places along
the route; also for rudimentary overnight shelter in halls.  Marchers
are recommended however to come equipped with food, eating utensils and
mugs, and sleeping-bags or blankets.  If there is a sufficiently large
turnout of marchers, return transport from Aldermaston to Reading on
Monday (early evening) will be arranged.

There will be a vigil at the main entrance to the plant day and night
for a week following the Monday demonstration.

Please fill in this form and return it to:-
The Secretary, Committee for Direct Action Against Nuclear War,
3 Blackstock Rd., London N.4. (tel. STA 2262)

----------------------------------------------------------------

I shall march all 4 days from Traf. Sq. to Aldermaston------------

I shall march on Friday from Traf. Sq. to Hounslow---------------

I shall march on Saturday from Hounslow to Maidenhead-----------

I shall march on Sunday from Maidenhead to Reading-------------

I shall march on Monday from Reading to Aldermaston----------

I could offer First Aid services en route--------------------

I have a motor vehicle (specify what sort) for accompanying---------

I could perform in---------produce------------a band or choir

I could keep vigil at Aldermaston from-------till--------on------
I could offer hospitality at----------------------------
I enclose----------to help defray costs of leaflets etc.

Name---------------Address----------------

Direct Action Committee against Nuclear War cyclostyled leaflet made to advertise the first march to Aldermaston in 1958 thought that popular resistance rather than top-down changes would achieve nuclear disarmament and unlike CND focused their efforts on disrupting the places where bombs were made and stored. Ideologically, *Peace News* was much closer to the DAC, but they had links with both organisations, particularly as the London branch of CND was based in 5 Cally Road.

Peace News' support for the growing nuclear disarmament movement led to increasing tensions with the Peace Pledge Union, the paper's host organisation. The nuclear disarmament movement was broad and did not have a uniformly pacifist position, focusing on the single issue of nuclear weapons rather than the overall abolition of war. Harry Mister remembered that some of those involved in *Peace News* thought the new movement 'the most likely source of new pacifists that existed in the land', while the PPU 'thought it was a diminution of pacifist ideals and they were not prepared to work with people who did not completely oppose war'.[16]

With some of those involved in *Peace News* deeply embedded in the DAC, including the paper's editor Hugh Brock, arguments developed on the *Peace News* board. In 1958 Sybil Morrison, a veteran pacifist and one of the first women to join the PPU, gave up her position as chair of the board because 'she was unhappy about the policy of the paper which she felt appeared to be the organ of [the] Campaign for Nuclear Disarmament and Movement for Colonial Freedom, whilst giving insufficient support to the Peace Pledge Union.'[17] Tensions continued to grow and by 1961 *Peace News* and the PPU agreed to separate. For *Peace News*, this meant it had greater independence but lost the backing of a larger organisation.

After several more demonstrations and a group trespass in Aldermaston in 1958, the DAC focused on the Thor rocket base at North Pickenham, near Swaffham, Norfolk. Here they organised an intensive campaign aiming to win support from the local trade unions and to persuade individual workers, contractors and suppliers to stop working with the base. They then held two direct actions at the missile base. On the first they were able to invade the base, while the second time they found it better defended and sat down to block the entrance. On this second occasion 45 arrests were made, with 30 people, including Michael Randle, Hugh Brock, Ian Dixon and Peace News assistant editor Christopher Farley held in prison for a fortnight when they refused to agree to 'hold the peace.' This was Michael Randle's first prison sentence, which he said was 'something I had anticipated and felt to be in the tradition of Gandhian direct action. At that level, it was very satisfying to feel one was part of that tradition.'

16   Interview with Harry Mister by Alan Dein for King's Cross Voices.

17   '*Peace News* Directors Minutes March 27 1958',

University of Bradford Special Collections, Archives of *Peace News* Cwl/PN/1/2.

## Committee of 100 ·

5 Cally Road was developing into the 'movement centre' Harry Mister had hoped it would be. The *Peace News* office was used by other groups to contact the press about their actions, using lists of sympathetic journalists and pre-addressed envelopes kept ready for urgent communiques.[18] Rooms in the building were rented to groups for their meetings, which helped to raise funds for the building. Tony Weaver, who became a Housmans company member and joined its publications committee around this time, remembered 'this was a period of very vital associations at 5 Caledonian Road between *Peace News*; CND London Region, which used to meet there throughout the night it seemed, to organise the early Aldermaston marches; and the Committee of 100.'[19]

The Committee of 100 was an attempt to combine the direct action approach of the Direct Action Committee with the mass participation achieved by CND. The idea for the committee developed in discussions between Ralph Schoenman, a postgraduate student, Hugh Brock and April Carter from the DAC and Alan Lovell, Stuart Hall and Ralph Miliband, who were all prominent figures in the New Left.

The Committee of 100 was launched in October 1960, with a hundred members, or signatories, which was meant to limit individual liability for the actions it organised. Many of the 100 were well-known people, who lent their names to the organisation but did not necessarily take an active part. Pacifist philosopher Bertrand Russell became the committee's figurehead, stepping down as President of CND to take up the same role for the Committee of 100. Michael Randle became its secretary. They planned to call for a mass campaign of civil disobedience using Gandhian methods of non-cooperation, challenging the government to 'fill the jails'.

The first public action of the Committee of 100 was on 18 February 1961 outside the Ministry of Defence. It was Britain's first ever large-scale sit-down protest, with an estimated 5,000 people taking part. Michael Randle remembered the day:

One of the stipulations for the first Committee of 100 demonstration was, it would not go ahead unless we got a minimum of 2,000 people pledging to take part in the sit-down. And it was going to be a sit-down outside the Ministry of Defence, the back of Whitehall. And that did go ahead and was very well attended. In the end we got about 5,000 people. We blocked it for a couple of hours. But the police didn't intervene, there were no arrests.

There was one little piece of drama where, taking a leaf out of Martin Luther's book, we worked out an anti-nuclear declaration, and I had that printed up, and [with the Reverend Michael Scott] tried to nail it to the Ministry of Defence door in Whitehall.

18    *Peace News*, '*Peace News* Annual Report 1960–61', University of Bradford Special Collections, Archives of *Peace News* Cwl/PN/2.

19    Tony Weaver, 'Farewell Note to Housmans Board', 12 September 1989, Housmans Archive, Housmans Minute Book 1990–95.

# TRIUMPH FOR COMMITTEE OF 100

LAST Saturday's sit-down outside the Ministry of Defence in London was joined by about 4,000 people, apart from several thousand supporters who added their solidarity.

This act of mass civil disobedience, organised by the Committee of 100, demanded "the complete rejection by our country of nuclear weapons and all policies and alliances that depend upon them." It was aimed especially at the Polaris agreement with the USA.

The Committee's declaration—which was posted on the Ministry's door, and is on page five of *Peace News*—concluded: "Our action today is the first step in a campaign of non-violent civil disobedience. We hereby serve notice

### INSIDE

## BERTRAND RUSSELL

explains why Britain should get out of NATO and adopt a policy of neutralism

*page nine*

## PAGES OF PICTURES

of last Saturday's sit-down in London outside the Ministry of Defence

*pages five-eight*

photo: Austin Underwood

on our Government that we can no longer stand aside while they prepare to destroy mankind."

The entire protest, including the march from Marble Arch to Trafalgar Square, the big rally there and the sit-down itself, was marked by a striking calm seriousness of purpose. The only opposition came from a handful of fascist and Mosleyites who turned out to shout for the Bomb.

But it was also a great *human* protest. Some demonstrators had given up their jobs in order to be free to go to jail. One young mother had checked with the authorities that she would be able to keep her baby with her if she were imprisoned.

The chief marshal was handed an envelope containing this anonymous message: "We must have supreme courage in our convictions. We must give our time, our money, even our freedom. We must succeed." The envelope also contained 20 £5 notes.

Austin Underwood's picture, right, shows the sit-down in progress down one side of the Ministry of Defence.

### ... and the police did not arrest a single demonstrator

"And so disobedience—deliberate, proclaimed and placarded disobedience—to the laws of the State has still about it something of a defiance hurled at the gods, and provides, too, a test of how great their power really is. Cortes threw down the idols on the island of Cozumel to prove to the natives, by his impunity, that their gods were false. When Hampden refused to pay ship money at Charles I's behest, his friends trembled for him; but his escape was proof that celestial thunderbolts were no longer wielded by the Stuart King: the king fell. Ransack the history of revolutions, and it will be found that every fall of a régime has been presaged by a defiance which went unpunished. It is as true today as it was 10,000 years ago that a power from which the magic has gone out falls."—Bertrand de Jouvenel: "Power: The Natural History of its Growth."

---

I was trying to nail the declaration, and somebody came up from the Ministry of Defence, he said, 'You can't do that, that's an oak door. You can't start driving nails into it.' And then the police came and seized the hammer and nails. So, there was a true British compromise. We stuck it up on the door with Sellotape.

The paper sellotaped to the door of the Ministry of Defence said 'Our action today is the first step in a campaign of nonviolent civil disobedience. We hereby serve notice on our government that we can no longer stand aside while they prepare to destroy mankind.'[20]

The congenial atmosphere of the first sit down did not last long. When the Committee repeated the action on 29 April, more than 800 people were arrested.

20  *From Protest to Resistance: The Direct Action Movement against Nuclear Weapons*, Peace News Pamphlet, no. 2 (Nottingham: Mushroom, 1981), p. 45.

By August 1961, the world seemed closer than ever to nuclear war, with conflict worsening between the superpowers in Berlin and nuclear tests being carried out by both the Soviet Union and the USA. A new demonstration was called by the Committee of 100 for 17 September 1961 in Trafalgar Square. This time the government banned the protest and imprisoned thirty-two members of the Committee, including Bertrand Russell, when they refused to agree not to protest. The worsening global situation and publicity from the government crackdown made the demonstration larger than ever.

Diana Shelley, then eighteen years old, was one of those who defied the ban to join the demonstration. She had been brought up in in London by parents who were members of the Communist Party. Diana had already been on two Aldermaston marches but remembers the banned protest in Trafalgar Square as pivotal to her development as an activist:

> I didn't know why you wanted to go and sit down outside something. I didn't know what the point was about civil disobedience … So, how I then got involved was they called a demonstration for Trafalgar Square to march to the Air Ministry in September 1961. And it was banned … And [the Committee of 100 members] got hauled in and bound over to keep the peace if they didn't sign to say that they would not go on the demonstration.[21] And I was very, very shocked at such a terrible thing being done in terms of civil liberties. So, I went to that one, with some friends from school … And we sat in Trafalgar Square. The ban ran out at midnight, and we left, a lot of people left, and that was when the police moved in and arrested 1,341 people, the largest arrest on a civil disobedience demonstration.'

Around 12,000 people took part in the Trafalgar Square demonstration in defiance of the ban. Many of the arrests were violent, with reports of police throwing protesters into the fountains, dragging them along the floor and injuring them in the police stations.[22] Despite the violence experienced that night, the Committee of 100 seemed to be achieving its aims, it was filling the jails and provoking a response from the government.

Filled with confidence from this success, the Committee's next step was even more ambitious: they called for 50,000 people to pledge to take part in simultaneous actions at military bases on 9 December 1961. The bases targeted would be Wethersfield in Essex, Ruislip in Middlesex and Brize Norton in Oxford, plus mass civil disobedience demonstrations in Cardiff, Bristol, Yorkshire and Manchester.

---

21   In Samantha Carroll's thesis on the Committee of 100 she describes how over thirty-six Committee of 100 members were summoned to court to be bound over to keep the peace. Thirty-two refused to do so. Unless they agreed to be bound over, those summoned were given prison sentences of between one and two months. Betrand Russell and his wife had their sentences shortened to seven days due to fears for their health.

22   Samantha Jane Carroll, '"Fill the Jails": Identity, Structure and Method in the Committee of 100, 1960 – 1968' (unpublished Doctoral thesis (DPhil), University of Sussex, 2011 <http://sro.sussex.ac.uk/id/eprint/6910/>.

In response, the government announced that any invasion of military bases would be in contravention of the Official Secrets Act, which could lead to long prison sentences for those arrested. Newspapers reported that 'guards might shoot' and the bases were fortified with new fences and warning signs.[23] Then, the day before the demonstration, five of the organisers were arrested: Helen Allegranza, Terry Chandler, Ian Dixon, Trevor Hatton and Michael Randle. With Pat Pottle, who went on the run until a few days before the trial and then reappeared to defend himself in court, they became known as the 'Wethersfield Six'. They were charged with two counts of conspiracy under Section One of the Official Secrets Act, which was concerned with espionage. These were serious charges that could result in lengthy prison sentences: in theory there was no upper limit to the sentences that could be given for conspiring to contravene the Official Secrets Act.

Despite the risk of arrest and imprisonment, 7,000 people attended the various protests, although this number fell far short of the 50,000 they had aimed for. Over 800 arrests were made.

The trial of the Wethersfield Six absorbed much of the Committee's energy. At the end of the trial in February 1962, the five male defendants were sentenced to eighteen months in prison, while Helen Allegranza, the only woman on trial, was given a year. The long prison sentences were by no means easy for the activists and their families, for instance Michael Randle's first child was born while he was imprisoned. Helen Allegranza had a particularly difficult time. As the only woman she was imprisoned alone in the high security women's prison, Holloway, while her co-defendants were imprisoned together in men's prisons, and at least some of the time in open prisons. Although it is not possible to know how connected this was to her experience of prison, not long after she was released Helen Allegranza took her own life.

After the trial the momentum behind the Committee of 100 was dissipating. While the Wethersfield Six were in prison direct action at military bases continued, but the large numbers who attended the demonstrations the year before proved elusive. At the beginning of 1963 Bertrand Russell resigned as President of the Committee; many of the better-known signatories followed his lead and left.

The original idea behind the Committee had run its course, but this was not the end. It changed its structure, setting up local groups around the country. Michael Randle reflected that being part of the Committee of 100 had a 'radicalising influence' on some of the people involved.[24] Having gained experience of imprisonment and state repression in the first two years of the Committee, some members increasingly questioned whether the Gandhian principle of openness with the authorities was

23  Samantha Jane Carroll, p. 141.    24  *From Protest to Resistance*, p. 23.

the right approach. In 1962 while on the run, Pat Pottle had argued that he was of more use outside prison than in it. He said that the Committee should only tell the authorities their plans if that was the most effective thing to do: 'we are not conducting a protest movement, but a resistance struggle against the State machine'.[25]

In February 1963, at a Committee of 100 conference, a statement entitled 'Beyond Counting Arses', signed by eight committee members with connections to the libertarian socialist group Solidarity, was distributed. It stated:

> We started off as a movement against 'The Bomb'. This struggle has led us to realise that our opponent is the state itself, and the social and economic interests it protects.[26]

Beyond Counting Arses argued that the Committee's signature tactic of a mass sit down had become ritualistic. Success was evaluated by the size of the write up in the *Guardian*, or the numbers of 'arrested arses'. Instead, the authors argued that the Committee should widen the idea of direct action, taking a more subversive and less open approach to 'unmask and publicise' the government's preparations for war.

Not long afterwards, in April 1963, an anonymous group calling themselves 'Spies for Peace' did just that. They published a pamphlet 'Danger! Official Secret', revealing secret plans for the event of nuclear war, including the locations of a network of government bunkers that were intended to house up to 5,000 people, part of the Regional Seats of Government, who would govern the country from these bunkers in the event of nuclear war.

Diana Shelley explained how it felt to read the revelations at the time:

> It was genuinely very shocking, because the premise was that a nuclear war could be fought, and you would put your politicians and your civil servants into these bunkers, and they would survive the nuclear war, which of course was extremely unlikely, what would the radiation levels have been like when they came out ... But, you know, the bunker mentality was, well as long as we stay in here, we'll be all right. What we're going to breathe and eat is another problem, but still. But the general gist of it was we don't give a damn about the peasants out there, they can fry.

The pamphlet was ready in time for the annual Aldermaston march. It included a map of the location of one of the bunkers, RSG-6, which was just off the route of the march and challenged the marchers to split off from the main march to visit it. A significant

25  *From Protest to Resistance*, p. 37.
26  'Beyond Counting Arses | Libcom.Org' <https://libcom.org/library/beyond-counting-arses> [accessed 12 May 2022].
27  *Peace News*, 19 April 1963.
28  The Spies for Peace were never caught but some of them chose to reveal themselves in oral history interviews with Samantha Carroll decades later. A detailed account of the Spies for Peace can be read in Carroll's article, 'Danger! Official Secret: The Spies for Peace: Discretion and Disclosure in the Committee of 100', *History Workshop Journal*, 69.1 (2010), 158–76 <https://doi.org/10.1093/hwj/dbp032>.

# The spies were right

On Thursday, April 11, a pamphlet entitled "Danger Official Secret RSG 6" was circulated to the national press, political parties, prominent personalities in the peace movement including Bertrand Russell, Albert Schweitzer and Linus Pauling, to a number of MPs and to MI5. The pamphlet gave details of the Government's plans for setting up 12 regional seats of government (RSGs) in secret underground offices, naming the sites of several of them and giving names and telephone numbers. It also gave details of the results of the military exercises Parapluie and Fallex 62 which showed that a nuclear attack would reduce this country to chaos.

A Government official was quoted by the "Daily Express" on April 13 as saying : "The location of these centres is an official secret and this document could be of value to spies. The information is restricted to certain Government departments concerned with defence." The accuracy of the pamphlet was not called into question.

As "Peace News" went to press this week Special Branch were reported to be still making enquiries about the source of the pamphlet.

*Peace News* welcomes the publication of the Spies for Peace pamphlet and considers it to have been in the national interest. It is a valuable supplement to the Black Paper which we published on the effects of nuclear war, because it shows that the Government is well aware of the total chaos that war will bring, but is trying to withhold this from the public.

The really important revelation in the document concerns the effects in Britain of the Fallex 62 NATO exercise in September, 1962. The Defence White Paper for 1963-4 states: "In the course of participating last autumn in the NATO Exercise Fallex 62 the opportunity was taken to practise our mobilisation plans, and to exercise procedures for co-operation with the civil authorities in home defence. . . . In general the exercise showed that the plans were basically sound and practicable." The Spies for Peace pamphlet shows on the contrary that the exercise proved that a nuclear attack would result in complete chaos:

"The medical services broke down completely. Every hospital in the Southern Region was destroyed or put out of action by fall-out, the death of doctors, or lack of supplies. The communications system broke down and the roads were choked. Gloucester, Oxford and Plymouth were eliminated by small bombs. London was paralysed; to go above ground was death. A lethal belt of radiation extended as far out as Windsor. Three-quarters of the police in the Southern Region were killed, injured or irradiated. Losses among the civilian population were proportionately even higher. Whoever won the war, we lost it."

This confirms the report on Fallex 62 published by Der Spiegel last October and reprinted in *Peace News* November 9.

policy. Certainly there can be no justification on grounds of security or anything else for the Government to deceive the public in defiance of its own avowed policy.

The Labour opposition could make much of the Government's deception of the public. Unfortunately they are so committed to the arms programme that they seem more likely to use the opportunity to attack the Government for not taking even stricter security precautions.

The Spies for Peace pamphlet also gives details, including telephone numbers and addresses, of the 12 underground Regional Seats of Government that would be set up in the event of war. The general outline of the plan for Regional Commissioners had already been made public. What the pamphlet does is to show in some detail the sort of powers that such Regional Governments would have, assuming that the plan worked out and that there were still other people left alive to govern. Regional Commissioners would have absolute power in their regions and would have under them an administrative staff in which the main departments of government would be represented - the Army, Navy, Air Force, police, etc. It would in fact be a completely authoritarian administration, governing by decree.

More important is the fact that the system of Regional Governments could only operate at all if the nuclear attack was on an absurdly small scale. A large scale attack, which seems more probable, would leave the Regional Government in charge of several million corpses for the few weeks it might hope to survive itself.

The picture that emerges from the pamphlet is this: the Government are spending millions of pounds on a system of regional military dictatorships, to operate from

or the details of the Fallex 62 operation. It is a frightening reminder of the totalitarian implications of nuclear war preparations and of the way they have come already to be accepted as necessary in the national interest.

Instead the press has concentrated its attack on the irresponsibility of the authors of the pamphlet. They suggest that by naming the location of the Regional Seats of Government the authors pinpoint new nuclear targets for an enemy and thus render a genuinely defensive system inoperable. This is not a very serious point. The pamphlet states that 5,000 people are involved in the plans for Regional Government and thousands more workers and administrators must know of the existence of the sites. It is inconceivable that the Russians are unaware of their existence, even if they do not know exactly what is going on in them. Several newspapers, in fact, point out that national security was not vitally affected by the publication of the addresses of the sites; bomber and rocket

defence programme is part and parcel of the nuclear system. As the Defence White Paper states:

"These plans (for civil defence) which provide for the close co-operation of the civil and military authorities are an integral part of our defence plans."

From time to time reports circulate about massive dispersal plans in the Soviet Union in the event of nuclear attack, and these, in conjunction with its nuclear arms programme, are invariably seen as evidence of sinister designs. The irony of the present situation is that the more thorough a nuclear armed government's plans for civil defence are, the more nervous its opponents will be that an attack is impending.

A neutralist government could not possibly have a system of secret underground centres, if only because secret operations would completely destroy the confidence of other countries in its sincerity. It would either have to provide an enormously costly deep-shelter programme or rely on its posi-

number of people did just that, to the dismay of some of the CND organisers.

The front page of the next issue of *Peace News* proclaimed, 'The Spies were Right'.[27] While the authorities searched for the elusive Spies for Peace, people all around the country were duplicating and re-typing the pamphlet to distribute it as widely as possible.[28]

Committee of 100 members re-focused their energies on new social and political campaigns in which they felt they could have a direct impact, using nonviolent direct action to campaign on issues ranging from housing to gay liberation. The committee's actions became increasingly theatrical, using stunt-like tactics that would become more widely used a few years later. The success of the early actions was never replicated after the arrests of the Wethersfield Six, but they had helped to popularise nonviolent direct action in Britain.

Ian Dixon reflected on the impact of those years:

Nonviolent direct action now is seen as almost mainstream. I mean Greenpeace do it, you know. The local squatting group do it. Everybody knows about civil disobedience. And I'm sure that was an awareness that was created very much due to people around 5 Cally.

NEWS
S IN NOTTINGHAM

ws, the anarchist-pacifist fort-
per, has now moved to Notting-

1973, four of the five editors at
roposed that the paper, then
ould be published fortnightly,
ain office to a midland town
tself offset-litho. After a pro-
bate, the paper went fortnightly

at Easter an
litho.

Now, after a
boat along
mented by a
in Nottingha
months, that
its own print
printed by F
ciated with
Foundation
Control.

pregnant wife of Ken Weller (who was also arrested), is
n the Greek embassy last Friday night after a group of
s had taken over the building. "The Save Greece Now!" and
on behalf of the people of Greece" and "against tyranny."
ple were arrested, though more than 50 took part - at least ten
a police van. (Photo: Syndication International).

5 1967 1s (US 25 cents)

## GENTLE AFFRAY

you!' —SCREAMS EMBASSY MAN

will con-
its new

artin Luther King, back
olstoy on Disarmament,
'ich's sexual revolution, p
on-violence in France, pa
page 14
drawal, p

# Peace News

633 Oct 13 1967 1s (US 25 cents)

Tony Smythe
IBERTY

### The Greek

People who break into embass
Greek one in London or a British one
should not expect diplomatic immunit
although a vote at the Labour Party con
this week shows that the political sympa
the party in power are broadly aligned w
anti-Patakos demonstrators whom Mr
Widgery sentenced on Wednesday, al
British citizen would prefer such
decided on judicial rather than politica
But on this occasion there is serious doub
judicial criteria have been properly appli

It was reasonable of the judge to
that the Upper Brook Street demon
April was not wholly spontaneous. Bu
demonstrations spontaneity is general
for far greater public disorder than
this occasion. The judge selected Ter
and Michael Randle—two contumacio
and anti-nuclear prison graduates—
treatment, justifying the sentences
on the conventional police court grou
had been "in trouble before." Bo
ouble was their share in t

# CHAPTER 2

# REVOLUTIONARY PROJECTS

## *Peace News* adjusts

After 1963, the activists grouped around *Peace News* and 5 Cally Road had to adapt to the nuclear disarmament movement shrinking rather than expanding. There were internal changes for *Peace News*, one being the resignation of Hugh Brock as editor in 1964. Hugh Brock had led *Peace News* since 1955, while also being deeply involved in the nonviolent direct action movement for nuclear disarmament. His departure marked the end of an era for the paper.

The next editor was Ted Roszak, an American academic who would later coin the term 'counterculture'. Although he stayed only a year in the role, Ted Roszak implemented ambitious changes at *Peace News*. He oversaw a modernist redesign of the paper, brought in paid contributors and published more articles on the arts and social and political issues.

There were new, younger staff members recruited to work on the paper. One was Bob Overy, who joined in 1965. He remembered it as an exciting time:

> We had flower power ... the [outrage against the] Vietnam War, ... the civil rights movement in the States, and still the direct action movements in Britain ... And I was on the edge of all sorts of things, wrote regularly in the paper, and got very interested in nonviolence. So that was a fascinating time.

In 1965 the chair of the *Peace News* board, author Vera Brittain, stood down from her post, saying that she finally felt the time was right to focus on her writing, as the argument about nuclear disarmament had been won:

> Though we can't pretend that nuclear weapons are conquered, most people feel morally about them in the way that pacifists do and differ rather in *how* to end the threat rather than the need to end it.[1]

Meanwhile, the older activists who had led *Peace News* in the late 1950s and early 1960s and remained on the board, were worried that nonviolence seemed to be falling out of favour with radical political movements around the world. The war in Vietnam was the main issue for peace activists for much of the 1960s, but the large anti-war

1   Vera Brittain, 'Letter from Vera Brittain to Harry Mister', 1 January 1965, University of Bradford Special Collections, Archives of *Peace News* Cwl/PN/3/4.

2   'Minutes of *Peace News* Board Meeting 5 March 1966', University of Bradford Special Collections, Archives of *Peace News* Cwl/PN/3/4.

3   'Memo Entitled 'Some Comments on Ted Roszak's "Some Thoughts on the Crisis in Circulation", 1964', University of Bradford Special Collections, Archives of *Peace News* Cwl/PN/3/2.

4   'Minutes of *Peace News* Annual General Meeting 21 May 1966', University of Bradford Special Collections, Archives of *Peace News* Cwl/PN/5.

5   Harry Mister, 'Harry Mister's Report to *Peace News* Board Meeting 1 May 1965', University of Bradford Special Collections, Archives of *Peace News* Cwl/PN/3/4.

6   'Minutes of *Peace News* Board Meeting 4 December 1965', University of Bradford Special Collections, Archives of *Peace News* Cwl/PN/3/4.

7   'Minutes of *Peace News* Board Meeting 4 December 1965'.

demonstrations were not always nonviolent. Unlike many groups on the Left, pacifists did not support the armed resistance of the North Vietnamese. In response to Che Guevara's call for 'many Vietnams', they called for an end to the war and for 'no more Vietnams'. In 1966 the *Peace News* board asked actor Vanessa Redgrave to resign from her post as Chair because she supported Vietnam's armed resistance.[2] She had only been appointed to the role to replace Vera Brittain a year earlier.

In the mid-1960s, *Peace News* debated what the paper's purpose should be and who its readership was. Was it a news service for the peace movement, or did it have its own mission? Was the paper's priority to speak to its traditional core audience of pacifists, many of whom were now aging, or did they need to recruit a new, younger audience?

Vera Brittain complained that although the paper had separated from the Peace Pledge Union, 'the "ghetto" mentality has persisted in a large percentage of our readers. These, as you will doubtless have judged from the correspondence that comes in, demand that PN shall limit itself to news of the "peace movement" ... and deal mainly with "pacifism" — i.e., the old slogans and cliches which became outdated as soon as the nuclear age began.'[3]

Rod Prince, editor from 1965 to 1967, agreed that *Peace News* should have a broader remit. He wanted the paper to 'stress the things people could do to change the circumstances of their lives: in face of the strong grip of the war system on people's minds, they need both the means to act nonviolently for change, and the confidence that they can succeed. This was why *Peace News* placed special emphasis on developments like the Factory for Peace, the Civil Rights movement in the USA, community action on subjects like housing, and developments in the arts which can change people's consciousness and increase their social understanding.'[4]

Sales were down by a third in 1965. Circulation was only 7,300, significantly less than in the difficult days immediately after the Second World War.[5] *Peace News* relied on the profits from Endsleigh Cards and Housmans to keep afloat, but profits from the Christmas cards had diminished, mainly because the idea of charity cards had proved so popular they were now being made by others. Housmans was steadily growing, mainly by selling stationery and providing printing services to local businesses, but this was not enough to keep the newspaper solvent. The price of *Peace News* was raised, but still the fall in sales meant they needed to make savings of £6,000 at the end of 1965.[6] The *Peace News* board debated how best to respond to their worsening financial crisis.

Harry Mister advocated economising by cutting jobs and asking the remaining staff to accept a greater workload and 'a more austere framework within which to operate'.[7] Ted Roszak protested that Harry's suggestion 'sounds like a proposal for a pacifist monastery'. Rather than attempt to continue under these conditions, he argued, *Peace News* should close if it did not have enough support to continue.[8] The immediate crisis was averted through a fundraising drive that raised enough to cover the deficit, but the wider financial problem, and the expectation that people work for low salaries, continued.

In 1967 Rod Prince resigned as editor after just over two years in the job. His reasons included 'a general sense of mental and emotional exhaustion with regard to the paper', feeling dispirited about the state of the movement, not being willing to work evenings and weekends and wanting more money.[9] The other editorial staff, Bob Overy, Roger Barnard and Peter Willis, proposed that they take over the role of editor jointly, as a collective. They would keep their distinct roles as news editor and features editor, for example, but make decisions about the paper together. This, Bob argued in a memo to the board, would make the paper more democratic.[10] Their proposal was accepted, and they formed the first editorial collective to run *Peace News*, recruiting a fourth worker to replace Rod Prince.

## Greek Embassy Occupation

In the same period, *Peace News* and 5 Cally Road remained connected to the Committee of 100, who continued to campaign on a growing number of issues. One of these was the situation in Greece, as Bob remembered:

> A peace movement started that was calling for Greece to leave NATO, and to abandon nuclear weapons, or nuclear alliance. And we, Committee of 100 people, got very involved in that issue, and went over to support them on their marches. And so that then became a bond. And I was the reporter who was keeping us in touch on the Greek issue and talking to the organisation in London that represented the Greek left and the Greek radicals. Which was an absolutely amazing movement to be part of.

The Committee of 100 had formed the Save Greece Now campaign to protest the Greek monarch's state visit to London in 1963. Then, on 21 April 1967, a military coup took place in Greece. A meeting was quickly called by Committee of 100 and Direct Action Committee members in the basement of 5 Cally Road. They planned an occupation of the Greek Embassy in London in response to the coup. Occupying an embassy was a daring move, and as the embassy was technically foreign soil, there

8   'Memo from Ted Roszak' Special Collections, Archives of *Peace News* Cwl/PN/3/4.

9   'Editor's Statement to Board from Rod Prince, July 18th, 1967', University of Bradford Special Collections, Archives

of *Peace News* Cwl/PN/3/6.

10  Bob Overy, '*Peace News* Board Memo', 1967, University of Bradford Special Collections, Archives of *Peace News* Cwl/PN/3/6.

was some debate about whether British law would apply.

Diana Shelley remembered:

What happened was, somebody hired a removal van, and about fifty of us got into it, probably from King's Cross but I can't remember that. And we drove then to Upper Brook Street where the Greek Embassy was then, in Mayfair. The removal van pulled up outside

---

# Peace News

1610 May 5 1967 1s (US 25 cents)

# 'In Greece we would shoot you!'

## —SCREAMS EMBASSY MAN

## THE GENTLE AFFRAY

Gwyn Weller, pregnant wife of Ken Weller (who was also arrested), is removed from the Greek embassy last Friday night after a group of demonstrators had taken over the building. The Save Greece Now! movement was acting "on behalf of the people of Greece" and "against tyranny." Forty-two people were arrested, though more than 50 took part - at least ten escaped from a police van. (Photo: Syndication International.)

"In Greece, we would shoot you!" shouted a violently excited Greek attaché at the Greek embassy in London last Friday night, as police came pouring in.

His words, more than anything else, explain and justify the audacity of more than 50 supporters of the "Save Greece Now!" movement in attempting to deprive the military regime in Greece of its diplomatic office in Britain. If left-wingers can be dealt with so severely over there, the penalties in Britain for such extreme action as a non-violent coup seem suddenly acceptable and relatively unimportant.

Thoughts of this kind must have been in the minds of the participants as they moved quickly into the embassy in Upper Brook Street at 8 pm last Friday. The doorman claims to have been knocked down by those who rang the doorbell but, according to accounts from those involved, his story (so well-publicised by the press) is untrue. No doorman when faced with inquisitive police, press and a furious ambassador would have the courage to admit that he was fooled by a Greek girl with flowers and therefore offered no resistance to an entry party of fifty. But that is what really happened.

Similarly, the charge against Terry Chandler, that he assaulted a police officer, is a cover-story for the fact that he was himself assaulted by more than one policeman, as well as by the Greek attaché who lost control of himself. It is clear that the police would like to separate a few individuals from the 42 so as to bring serious charges that might stand up in a court of law. Terry Chandler is being victimised because he resisted arrest by holding on to stair-rails and bannisters as he was beaten and dragged out of the building.

One of the demonstrators, Ken Weller, said to a policeman who was hitting a girl: "I have your number. Let her alone." The policeman replied, "Oh, you do, do you," and hit him twice in the stomach. As he was being taken downstairs, he commented to another policeman, "Don't you remember Challenor?" He was then grabbed, but said: "I've got your number too." For this he was kicked several times in the genitals: "Do you still remember my number?", said the second policeman. "I've forgotten," was the reply. The

up to serious examination. The demonstrators, to the best of our knowledge, used no violence whatsoever. What is more, the damage done to embassy property was done by the police as they broke into the building rather than by the demonstrators locking and barricading doors. In any case, the charges refer to what happened *in the road*, that is, in Upper Brook Street, rather than in the embassy, and the demonstrators were in the road only as they ran quickly into the embassy and as they were dragged, non-resisting, out again to police vans. (The Greek embassy is legally Greek soil and so the British police cannot bring charges for what happened on Greek territory.)

Thus one is forced to believe that the serious affray charge, which surely cannot be found proved in any British court of law, however biased is police evidence, was brought in either to intimidate the magistrate into refusing bail last weekend and frighten the defendants, or, (assuming the charge isn't dropped in the meantime) to intimidate an Old Bailey jury into finding the defendants guilty on the lesser charge.

And what this means is that the police recognise this demonstration for what it was: a well-executed audacious action carried out by a group of people who are serious in their ideas of resistance to injustice even including an injustice as enormous and seemingly unchallengeable as the Greek military coup. George Brown (who had "recognised" the new Greek government on the day of the demonstration) was forced to apologise to the Greek ambassador for what had happened. He must be furious with the police for allowing it to happen. They must ensure that it doesn't happen again by getting savage sentences against the 42.

We don't know whether the "Save Greece Now!" movement and potential groups like it will be destroyed as the Committee of 100 was demoralised by the Wethersfield trial. But at the moment, morale seems high. We needn't expect another embassy to be taken over. (The rumours that there were ever any plans to kidnap the Greek ambassador are totally false.) But, whatever happens in the future, one way forward has been shown. Audacity is the key.

## Political prisoners back on death island

Bob Overy writes: "Everyone who got away is not living where he should be living," said Diana Pym, secretary of the League for Democracy in Greece, last Tuesday, describing the plight of left-wingers in Greece under the military regime.

have been "on the run." It is thought that Tony Ambatielos is still free. The League for Democracy in Greece is particularly anxious now because the island of "Gavdos," where the many detainees were said to have been taken, is in fact Yioura. Yioura

**Arrests and**

the embassy, and four people, two of them carrying daffodils ... knocked on the door, and the door was opened by one of the staff. And then, the back door of the van was opened, and we all leapt out.

We sort of spread through the embassy, being very careful not to damage anything, or be rude to anybody, or harm anything, and all of that. And the police arrived 40 minutes

1633 Oct 13 1967 1s (US 25 cents)

## Tony Smythe
# CIVIL LIBERTY AND CIVIL DISOBEDIENCE

On Monday, October 9, the Guardian printed a letter from Tony Smythe, General Secretary of the National Council for Civil Liberties, concerning the Old Bailey trial of the Greek Embassy demonstrators. Among other things, he wrote that "A battery of archaic and irrelevant laws are being used to curb dissent. The wide discretion of the DPP, the courts, and the police is more often exercised with petulance than with justice. If this state of affairs is allowed to continue, protest, and perhaps progress, will become virtually impossible. I would like to hear from those of your readers who are concerned at these sentences." Here, he discusses the trial and the sentences, and quotes from letters he received in reply to his request.

As the Labour Party conference was passing a resolution against the Greek dictators in defiance of the Executive's advice, jail sentences were being passed at the Old Bailey.

Some people, including most of the delegates, prefer George Brown and others to handle their politics for them. One wonders what the Foreign Secretary will make of the resolution. Other people such as Michael Randle and Terry Chandler, influenced no doubt by the inability of political leaders to link their actions to any clear moral principles, prefer to do it themselves.

As pacifists and democrats, they demonstrated at the Greek Embassy. The Scandinavian governments demonstrated their concern at the Council of Europe. To date the British government has remained silent. Randle and Chandler received 12 and 15 months apiece; Del Foley got 6 months; the British government has not been charged.

We can see the stark contrast between two very different concepts of political action. The conventional way incurs no risks and no penalties.

The reaction of Labour delegates when told of the sentences was fairly typical: they were either sorry but unprepared to act, or said simply, "If people will break into Embassies, what can they expect?" A resolution, even if it were to be ignored by the government, was the beginning and end of their protest.

I do not believe that any of us can avoid responsibility for what took place at the Old Bailey, no more than the 41 demonstrators could avoid responsibility for what has been happening in Greece.

After my depressing experience at the Labour Party conference it was very gratifying and moving to receive a remarkable response to my letter in the *Guardian*. In the first post after publication, the NCCL received 30 letters of support from a wide variety of individuals. The indications are that many more are on the way. I can do no better than quote from some of the letters:

"One of the freedoms we are supposed to cherish is surely the freedom to demonstrate. But

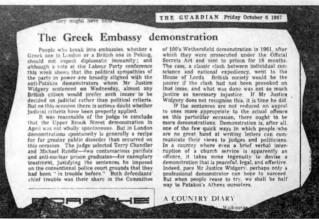

THE GUARDIAN   Friday October 6 1967

## The Greek Embassy demonstration

People who break into embassies, whether a Greek one in London or a British one in Peking, should not expect diplomatic immunity; and although a vote at the Labour Party conference this week shows that the political sympathies of the party in power are broadly aligned with the anti-Patakos demonstrators whom Mr Justice Widgery sentenced on Wednesday, almost any British citizen would prefer such issues' to be decided on judicial rather than political criteria. But on this occasion there is serious doubt whether judicial criteria have been properly applied.

It was reasonable for the judge to conclude that the Upper Brook Street demonstration in April was not wholly spontaneous. But in London demonstrations spontaneity is generally a recipe for far greater public disorder than occurred on this occasion. The judge selected Terry Chandler and Michael Randle—two contumacious pacifists and anti-nuclear prison graduates—for exemplary treatment, justifying the sentences he imposed on the conventional police court grounds that they had been "in trouble before." Both defendants' chief trouble was their share in the Committee

of 100's Wethersfield demonstration in 1961, after which they were prosecuted under the Official Secrets Act and sent to prison for 18 months. The case, a classic clash between individual conscience and national expediency, went to the House of Lords. British society would be the poorer if the clash had not been provoked on that issue, and what was done was not so much justice as necessary injustice. If Mr Justice Widgery does not recognise this, it is time he did.

If the sentences are not reduced on appeal to ones more appropriate to the actual offence on this particular occasion, there ought to be more demonstrations. Demonstration is, after all, one of the few quick ways in which people who are no great hand at writing letters can communicate their views to judges and politicians. In a country where even a brief interruption of a church service is apparently an offence, it takes some ingenuity to devise a demonstration that is peaceful, legal, and effective. Indeed, *pace* Mr Justice Widgery, perhaps only a professional demonstrator can hope to succeed. But when people cease to try, we shall be half way to Patakos's Athens ourselves.

A COUNTRY DIARY

Last Friday's "Guardian" editorial

## BOB OVERY
# Savage sentences in Greek Embassy trial

Terry Chandler: 15 months

If we call the prison sentences handed out at the Old Bailey last week "savage", that is also a reflection on the mentality of the judge. One wonders what primitive emotions passed through the mind of Mr Justice Widgery last Wednesday morning as he sentenced Terry Chandler, Michael Randle and Del Foley to jail for the invasion by

Michael Randle: 12 months

dants were fined between £20 and £100.

On Tuesday, the first day of the Old Bailey trial, when he heard what minimal evidence there was, Judge Widgery made it rather clear that he was seeking to judge us not on our political convictions about Greece, or even on our temerity in invading the Greek Embassy, but on our willingness

later ... I should explain that it was a very mixed group. A lot of us were Committee of 100 people with the kind of assumptions that had grown up for us during the '60s ... the LSE was having one of its first student occupations, and ... somebody went down and said, 'Oh look, there's going to be an occupation of the Greek Embassy.' And so, we had a lot of students as well.

**Bob Overy was there reporting for Peace News:**

I was a participant reporter, that was my concept of myself, that I wasn't a reporter who reported objectively from outside the action; I was a participant who reported what it was like to be part of the action. And so, the headline of the issue that came out after Greek Embassy was in quotes, 'In Greece We Would Shoot You!' That was my quote, of something that was said to me, when I was on a balcony, at the top of the staircase of the Greek Embassy, having run inside and then trying to occupy the place. And this guy actually went berserk, and I don't think he hit me, but he was certainly threatening to shoot me. He didn't produce a gun.

**The occupiers were arrested and removed from the embassy, but on the way to the police station some of them managed to escape, as Bob Overy recounted:**

I was a sort of purist nonviolent person, who once I was arrested, I'm arrested. This particular van load, they found that the police hadn't secured the door properly, and so they managed to get out of the van. So about fifteen people ... who had been taken away by van to the police station to be charged had got out and ran away. So, where I think I would have been far too goody-goody, you know, 'I'm going to take my Gandhian medicine,' they got away. And that was good for them.

**Forty-two people were arrested and charged with affray and threatening behaviour, one with assaulting a police officer. At committal proceedings, they faced different charges of riotous assembly and forcible entry: the latter was thrown out, and one defendant who had been arrested outside the embassy had his case dropped. As the group faced the prospect of a trial, Bob Overy wrote:**

We don't know whether the 'Save Greece Now!' movement and potential groups like it will be destroyed, as the Committee of 100 was demoralised by the Wethersfield trial. ... But, whatever happens in the future, one way forward has been shown. Audacity is the key.[11]

**At the trial a new charge of 'conspiracy to trespass' was added and the defendants faced a plea bargain. Reluctantly they pleaded guilty to the lesser charge of unlawful**

11    Bob Overy, '"In Greece We Would Shoot You!" Screams
Embassy Man', *Peace News*, 5 May 1967, 1610 edition, p. 1.

assembly to get the conspiracy and assault charges dropped. This meant no defence case was heard but the judge still gave significant prison sentences to those he decided were ringleaders on the basis of their prior convictions.

On 9 October 1967 Terry Chandler got fifteen months, Michael Randle twelve and Del Foley six.[12] Michael Randle, who by this time had two young children, remembered this imprisonment as 'a much tougher situation'. Michael Randle and Terry Chandler would still be in prison when the Committee of 100 wound up in 1968.

## The *Peace News* Collective

The group of editors now running *Peace News* saw the task of the paper as making the case for nonviolence and pacifism among the groups and individuals that made up the wider movement against war and for social change. The editors felt part of a new generation, with different ideas from the older group of activists who had opened 5 Cally Road a decade earlier.

In this period the paper now gave more space to social issues and grassroots community action projects. They covered the student activism of 1968, the democratic reforms and the subsequent Soviet invasion of Czechoslovakia the same year and continued to cover Vietnam. The paper took a leading role in reporting on the Nigerian civil war at a time when most of the British press ignored the British role in arming the Nigerian state to maintain its supply of oil from the country.[13] Bob Overy and Kevin McGrath both reported on the Northern Ireland civil rights movement, again as 'participant reporters'.

There were clearly some cultural differences between the younger and older people involved in *Peace News*. Some worried that the paper was losing its pacifist focus in favour of 'beatnikery', as one person who attended the 1966 *Peace News* AGM put it.[14] A review *Peace News* published of a banned erotic poetry book, *Golden Convolvulus*, caused controversy, with Harry Mister and others arguing it had lost the paper a considerable number of readers.[15] A memo to the *Peace News* Board argued that the paper's insistence on using 'four letter words' was 'gradually eroding the readership' and reducing the number of Christmas card orders.[16]

12  Bob Overy, 'Savage Sentences in Greek Embassy Trial', *Peace News*, 13 October 1967, 1633 edition.

13  Albert Beale, *Against All War: Fifty Years of Peace News 1936–1986*, A *Peace News* Pamphlet (Nottingham: *Peace News*, 1986).

14  'Minutes of *Peace News* Annual General Meeting 21 May 1966'.

15  'Minutes of *Peace News* Board Meeting 4 September 1965', University of Bradford Special Collections, Archives of *Peace News* Cwl/PN/3/4.

16  'Memo to *Peace News* Board from Arthur Taylor 5 January 1966', University of Bradford Special Collections, Archives of *Peace News* Cwl/PN/3/5.

# Peace News

659 April 12 1968 1s (US 25 cents)

# BRITAIN FOR SALE
page 5

Bob Overy recalled:

I do remember, as a young editor, going along to the annual fair. Harry was there and there was a famous guest who was there to open the fair ... I was introduced to this woman, and I didn't know anything about her. She was wearing a twin-piece and looked very old. And I found out later that it was Vera Brittain. I mean I think I knew at the time it was Vera Brittain, but I paid her no attention. Then of course I found out that she was a really significant person, who I should have paid a lot of respect to. And it just sort of shows, I think, that our attitude was that we were changing the world, and all these people had failed to deliver, and it was our turn, we were going to have a go, and go where they hadn't gone.

A memo Bob wrote in 1967 outlined the active approach he wanted the paper to take:

The job of *Peace News* is to define the areas in our society where nonviolent action is relevant and this must involve a close relationship with people who engage in this sort of action. One answer, then, is to spell out the urgent need for revolutionary projects and to associate ourselves in the planning of them, possibly outlining specific projects that should be taken up.[17]

In his interview with us he reflected:

What we did ... was to shift completely from a sort of tactical nonviolence ... to a more rounded view of nonviolence ... you did think about what it meant to be someone who was promoting nonviolence, and how that affected you. Rather than just being an academic thing, or a totally practical thing, it was actually a way of living.

In 1970, after several trips to Belfast as a reporter, Bob:

began to feel that what I was writing in the paper wasn't really the right place to be making my input, because what was happening on the ground over there, was where I wanted to be ... So, I decided to quit *Peace News* after five years, and go over there.

Bob and his partner went to live and work in the Shankill area of Belfast for two years, where they involved themselves in local community action in a working-class Protestant community.

As Bob had hoped, new groups were at times formed by the workers at *Peace News* in response to the issues they reported on, merging journalism and activism. In April 1971 Roger Moody, one of the co-editors of *Peace News* at the time, reported on the outbreak of civil war in what was then East Pakistan, which would lead to the independence of Bangladesh. Hundreds of thousands of people were killed and millions were displaced from their homes. Moody and others formed Operation Omega, which brought aid into Bangladesh, and continued to work in the area until 1973.

In 1971, a series of articles appeared in *Peace News* combining anti-militarism with ecology — 'Greenpeace — What *you* can do about your environment' — proved very popular. The next year in 1972 an extended article was published as a pull-out in *Peace News*, with thousands of copies reprinted and distributed.[18]

These articles inspired a new group, which would later become known as London Greenpeace. This was one of many Greenpeace groups which started around the world at this time (although London Greenpeace always remained independent). London Greenpeace used the War Resisters' International address at first, which was just next door at 3 Cally Road. The group's membership included people from *Peace News* and 5 Cally Road, including the paper's co-editor Howard Clark. Much later, in the late 1980s, the group would base its office at 5 Cally Road.

Albert Beale joined *Peace News* in 1972. From London originally, he had gone to Sussex University in the late 1960s where he started to define himself as a pacifist. He then moved back to London to join the staff of *Peace News*. He also got involved with the new Greenpeace group.

London Greenpeace's first campaign was against the French nuclear tests which had been held in the Pacific since the 1960s.[19] They organised a walk from London to Paris to protest against the tests. Albert remembered joining the walk to Paris in 1973, both to take part and to write about it for the paper:

> So, the plan was that ... a few dozen of us at least, would chain ourselves to pillars in the middle of Notre Dame [Cathedral in Paris] ... And the idea was that ... we were staying there long enough to ... do interviews with the international media before the CRS [French police] could arrest us. So, we did a deal with the church authorities that we would agree to release ourselves after a certain amount of time if they would keep the police at bay. I did an interview with the BBC World Service whilst rattling my chains in the Notre Dame ... it did the business, various of us who were in the church managed to talk to lots of media, and that was great.

Back in 5 Cally Road, Harry Mister agreed with the group of editors that the paper needed to help create a new pacifist movement, but he was keen that they did not alienate their older, more conventional readers in the process. He wrote 'I make no apology for going back to the original concept of the paper to serve all who are working for peace.'[20]

17   Bob Overy, '*Peace News* Board Memo'.
18   Beale, *Against All War*, p.38.
19   The tests did not conclude until the 1990s. A recent study shows 110,000 inhabitants of the Pacific were negatively affected by the radioactive fallout from these tests <https://www.bbc.co.uk/news/world-europe-56340159>

20   Harry Mister, 'The Future of Peace News', 1967, University of Bradford Special Collections, Archives of *Peace News* CwI/PN/3/6.

Bob commented:

When we were all being sort of ideologues upstairs, [Harry] was absolutely determined to keep the paper open and available to the old pacifists and the old CNDers, and all the reactionary peaceniks who were around the place. He wanted to sell the paper, and he didn't want us to have ideological disputes that meant that some people would stop reading the paper. So, he was interesting because he was always disappointed with what we were doing.

Harry Mister was general manager at 5 Cally Road, ultimately responsible for Housmans Bookshop, *Peace News* (although the editorial team ran the paper day-to-day) and Endsleigh Cards. He was involved at all levels in the work of the building, for instance he opened all the post and delivered *Peace News* to the wholesalers every week in his van. His family also helped out; his wife, Ivy Mister, did the accounts, and their children packed the Christmas cards every year. A sub-committee formed to review the low circulation of *Peace News* suggested that Harry was overloaded with work, that promotions work should be separated from business and that Harry should be relieved of day-to-day work like delivering the papers.[21] Most of their recommendations were not implemented.

Although Bob Overy saw his job at *Peace News* as an escape from the 'real world' he found that there was still a hierarchy at work in 5 Cally Road:

*Peace News* ... was elitist in a way. Because we [*Peace News* staff] were the university educated people who wrote long articles ... and had intellectual debates and all this stuff. Whereas, down in Housmans, you had a rather grubby bookshop with a number of volunteers, and a very few workers, who also worked very hard. But they were downstairs, and we were on the first floor, and there was a door to walk through between the two. That door rarely opened.

Unlike *Peace News*, Housmans was turning a profit, mostly through its commercial activities aimed at local people and businesses. Harry reported to the board's annual meeting in May 1967 that 'the shop is rather bursting at the seams and ways of extending it and improving the office arrangements are under consideration.'[22] It was still partly a peace movement bookshop and partly a commercial bookshop and stationers. They also published pamphlets and books about nonviolence and pacifism. Recent publications had included *Vietnam: The Dirty War*, *The Psychological Problem of Disarmament*, *Arms or Aid* and Allen Ginsburg's anti-war poem *Wichita Vortex Sutra*.

---

21    'Peace News Board Committee Report', 1967, University of Bradford Special Collections, Archives of *Peace News* Cwl/PN/3/6.

22    'Chairman's Report to the Annual Meeting of *Peace News* 6 May 1967', University of Bradford Special Collections, Archives of *Peace News* Cwl/PN/3/6.

The sub-committee's report in 1967 pointed out that some parts of Housmans work had a 'movement-service' function, but others were:

> strictly business ... and must therefore be dropped if they fail to make money ... We feel there is an uncertainty as to what the central function of Housmans is or should be. If its central function is to make money, it might be better for it to concentrate on stationery in view of the areas in which it is situated, and to carry only a small supply of strictly movement books. The alternative would be to build up Housmans as a bookshop specialising in a particular line of books.[23]

Jim Huggon, who worked in the bookshop from 1969 to 1982, had previously been involved in the Committee of 100. He was an anarchist as well as a pacifist and spoke regularly at Speakers' Corner in Hyde Park. Jim left his job as a teacher to work at Housmans, taking a significant pay cut. He remembered 'there were times when you'd sleep on the floor because you hadn't got the fare home'.

Jim, like some of the other bookshop staff, would have preferred Housmans to be a 'movement' bookshop, but the money Housmans made selling stationery, paperbacks and greeting cards was needed to finance *Peace News*.

In 1966, worried that the bookshop's funds were immediately swallowed up by *Peace News*' deficit, leaving them no money to run the bookshop, Harry Mister suggested separating Housmans and *Peace News* accounts.[24] In 1970, a company meeting thought about splitting the *Peace News* empire into four separate companies. The chairman, Geoffrey Tattersall, wrote to members describing the issues faced. The paper was losing its core supporters as they aged, financial difficulties were increasing and the new, younger staff were pushing for changes. Tattersall wrote:

> I have recently learnt a new name — 'participating democracy' which I gather means that the people who do the work shall control all the assets which they administer. For at least a year some of the staff have not been satisfied with just getting on with the work of publishing the paper, and there are several Directors who share their views.[25]

In keeping with this new mood, the paper became a full collective, meaning all staff would take part in decision-making. (Since 1967 there had been an editorial collective, but this did not include the other staff members who worked on the business side of the paper and did the important if routine work of managing subscriptions, sending out invoices and organising fundraising drives.) From December 1971 the masthead of *Peace News* proclaimed a new slogan:

23   '*Peace News* Board Committee Report'.

24   'Harry Mister's Report to *Peace News* Board Meeting 8 January 1966', University of Bradford Special Collections, Archives of *Peace News* Cwl/PN/3/5.

25   Geoffrey Tattersall, 'Letter from Geoffrey Tattersall, Chairman of *Peace News* to *Peace News* Members', 23 October 1970, University of Bradford Special Collections, Archives of Peace News Cwl/PN/3/7.

'for nonviolent revolution'.[26] The paper covered the counterculture and sexual politics, including the women's liberation movement and the newly formed Gay Liberation Front. Regular 'Potlatches' (an indigenous North American term for a gathering) were held to bring the paper's staff and readers together.

In 1971, *Peace News*, Housmans and the board (*Peace News* Trustees Ltd) all became separate companies. With Finsbury Park Typesetters, a sister company established in 1962 to typeset *Peace News* and raise money to subsidise the paper, they were now a group of four separate companies. Each of the three subsidiaries, *Peace News*, Housmans and Finsbury Park Typesetters, were overseen by *Peace News* Trustees. The trustees were a group of committed pacifists and veterans of the nonviolent direct action movement. They retained legal control of the group's property, including 5 Cally Road.

To enable *Peace News* to establish itself as an independent company the entire bank balance held by Housmans (£4,000) was transferred to pay off most of *Peace News'* debt (£4,600). The remaining debt of £600 was taken on by the trustees. Another £1,000 was withdrawn from Finsbury Park Typesetters, who also gave the paper a larger discount on typesetting. *Peace News'* offices at 5 Cally Road were provided rent free, while Housmans paid £500 a year to cover the costs of the building.[27]

However, despite this highly subsidised beginning as an independent company, *Peace News* ran up a new debt of £2,000 between April and October of 1971. One of the board members, Dennis Murray, proposed closing the paper down.[28] A seven-week-long Post Office strike from January 1971 had not helped, making it impossible to renew subscriptions to the paper or send out their annual appeal. However, even in normal times the paper was unable to pay for its production costs from its sales income, even when salary and office costs were excluded.[29] Despite there seeming to be no way out of its financial difficulties *Peace News* continued, subsidised by the other companies, some grant funding and its annual appeal to supporters.

Housmans now had more autonomy as a separate company. Their publishing arm had been discontinued due to the financial difficulties of the paper, but by 1973 the bookshop had published two new pamphlets, *Namibia* and a bibliography of Pacifism. One of the basement rooms was converted into 'Housmans Bookcellar' which was filled with peace movement literature, posters, pamphlets and books.

Meanwhile, *Peace News'* editors increasingly wanted more freedom and

26   Beale, *Against All War*, p.39.
27   Harry Mister, 'Behind the New *Peace News*', 1971, University of Bradford Special Collections, Archives of *Peace News* Cwl PN/3/8.
28   Dennis Murray, 'Letter from Dennis Murray to *Peace News* Trustees', 1 October 1971, University of Bradford Special

Collections, Archives of *Peace News* Cwl/PN/3/8.
29   In 1972 circulation was just 3,800 with 1,000 subscriptions included in that figure (Minutes of *Peace News* Trustees, November 18 1972, University of Bradford Special Collections, Archives of *Peace News* Cwl PN/3/8).

autonomy than they thought possible in 5 Cally Road. The differences came to a head in 1973, when four of the five editors of *Peace News* proposed that the paper should move outside London, that it should come out fortnightly instead of weekly, that it be printed offset litho and that the name should be changed.[30] A house was later offered to *Peace News* in Nottingham, at 8 Elm Avenue. *Peace News*' company members voted by eighteen to nine on 15 September 1973 in favour of all parts of the proposal apart from changing the name of the paper.[31]

This decision caused much debate between the trustees and the staff of *Peace News*, with many of the older board members like Hugh Brock firmly opposing the move and the end of a weekly paper. Arguing that a single editor should again be put in charge of the paper, Hugh Brock declared 'only one person can steer a boat although many may sail it'.[32]

All the editors except one (Albert Beale) argued that London had an 'absence of community' which made them feel 'pretty rootless'. They wrote:

> We feel a change is necessary because *PN* needs to be radical in its very mode of production, needs to break with the centralist habit of being based in London, needs to have more thought on the spot about content and presentation, needs to have staffies integrating living and working.

It would help that living costs and printing would both be cheaper outside of London.[33]

Albert Beale, alone among the editors, opposed the move. With others he started planning a new weekly paper based in London, which they hoped would 'reach out to larger numbers and to play more of a campaigning role'.[34] He explained that at the time:

> I thought on balance [the move] wasn't the best thing to do. I felt that one of the problems was that *PN* and people around *PN* were getting involved in quite sort of mainstream, national political struggles and so I didn't think the best thing for *PN* was to go away from that.

On 21 June 1974, an issue of *Peace News* reported that it had arrived in Nottingham and was now an 'anarchist-pacifist fortnightly paper'.[35] After a ten-day journey on

---

30  'The Proposal as Revised since April by Howard Clark, John Hyatt, Ian Kennard and Phil Reardon', University of Bradford Special Collections, Archives of *Peace News* Cwl PN/3/9.

31  Harry Mister, 'Letter from Harry Mister to *Peace News* Company Members', 1973, University of Bradford Special Collections, Archives of *Peace News* Cwl/PN/3/9.

32  Hugh Brock, 'Memo from Hugh Brock to Members of *Peace News* Ltd', 1973, University of Bradford Special

Collections, Archives of *Peace News* Cwl/PN/3/9.

33  'The Proposal as Revised since April by Howard Clark, John Hyatt, Ian Kennard and Phil Reardon'.

34  London *Peace News* Working Group, 'Continuing a London Based Newspaper: A Preliminary Statement of Intent', University of Bradford Special Collections, Archives of *Peace News* Cwl PN/3/9.

35  'Peace News Arrives in Nottingham', *Peace News*, 21 June 1974.

### PEACE NEWS ARRIVES IN NOTTINGHAM

*Peace News*, the anarchist-pacifist fortnightly paper, has now moved to Nottingham.

In March 1973, four of the five editors at the time proposed that the paper, then weekly, should be published fortnightly, move its main office to a midland town and print itself offset-litho. After a protracted debate, the paper went fortnightly at Easter and began to be printed offset-litho.

Now, after a 10-day journey by narrowboat along canal and River Trent, augmented by a van trip, it has set up office in Nottingham. For at least the next six months, that is until *Peace News* sets up its own printshop, the paper will be printed by Russell Press, the press associated with the Bertrand Russell Peace Foundation and the Institute for Workers' Control.

The editorial group has written: "By publishing once a fortnight and by moving out of the big city, it will be possible for us to become more closely in dialogue with people making social change in Britain. We want more people to make use of *Peace News* — by writing for it, by getting information from it, by selling it ...

"We believe that the creation of an alternative society, the development of radical forms of community action, and changes in personal life-style are central to the prospects for nonviolent revolution in Britain. The paper will still be concerned with campaigns against militarism, apartheid and social injustice, but its main emphasis has changed. Now there will be more reports on constructive projects and struggles for community control; we want to relate personal experience and living to politics; we are making our style of working reflect our philosophy more closely."

The paper will still have one person working out of 5 Caledonian Rd, London N1 (01-837 9794) — the old office. Part of that building will also be used by a group making preparations for producing a complementary pacifist weekly paper. If it is decided that this is feasible, a weekly paper may be launched in the autumn. Housmans Bookshop will continue on the ground floor, with its new bookcellar below.

The current issue of *Peace News* has been produced amidst all the chaos of moving.

**Contact: Peace News, 8 Elm Avenue, Nottingham. 0602-53587.**

LEFT: *Peace News*, 21 June 1974

a narrowboat called Bilster that transported *Peace News*' staff and possessions from 5 Caledonian Road — 'it may take longer but it'll be better for the earth, our souls and our pocket' — they arrived in their new home.[36] Moving to Nottingham, they wrote in *Peace News*, would make it possible for them to be:

> more closely in dialogue with people making social change in Britain ... Now there will
> be more reports on constructive projects and struggles for community control; we want
> to relate personal experience and living to politics; we are making our style of working
> reflect our philosophy more closely.[37]

Despite much work, by the end of 1974 the proposed London paper was not successful in securing funding and the idea never got off the ground. *Peace News* would keep a small office in 5 Cally Road as a foothold for their London worker but would not return fully to the building for another twenty years.

36   'Progress Report from the Nottingham Group', University of Bradford Special Collections, Archives of *Peace News* Cwl/PN/3/9.

37   '*Peace News* Arrives in Nottingham'.

RIGTH: Against the Law? Committee of 100: a legal handbook

against The Law?

OMMITTEE OF 100
legal hand book 1/-

can either order your re-arrest and sentence you to prison or order that your goods be distrained upon. (But please note earlier remarks under heading **Non-co-operation** about the position of those refusing name and address). At any time during these proceedings you can decide to pay the fine. It can also be paid for you either with or without your consent.

**Prison.** Prison without the option of a fine or binding over is not likely except in the case of the more serious charges.

### PENALTIES FOR LESS SERIOUS OFFENCES

The less serious offences carry maximum fines of between 40/- and £5. However, the magistrate can always order you to be bound over.

### PENALTIES FOR MORE SERIOUS OFFENCES

These offences carry heavy maximum penalties of up to several years' imprisonment. If you are charged with one of these offences you should make no statement and ask to contact a solicitor immediately.

In view of the large numbers of people involved we think it unlikely that more serious charges will be pressed except possibly in the case of some of the organisers.

### YOUNG PERSONS & JUVENILES

**Young persons** (17-21 years old) are dealt with in a Magistrates' Court in the same way as adults, but if imprisoned they are segregated from adult prisoners.

**Juveniles** (under 17 years old) are dealt with by Juvenile Courts. They cannot be imprisoned. A parent or guardian must be present at the court hearing and is responsible for the payment of any fines imposed.

### OPEN PRISONS

Faced with thousands of extra prisoners the authorities may decide to send many demonstrators to open prisons to relieve overcrowding. There are many more amenities in open prisons but they provide the Government with an easy means of coping with thousands of political prisoners—by in effect securing the prisoners' co-operation in their own detention.

You may decline to go to an open prison if you wish or explain that you will walk out if sent to one.

Published by
**THE COMMITTEE OF 100**
**13 GOODWIN STREET**
**LONDON N.4**
ARChway 1239

COMMITTEE
OF 100

Resistance
9 December, 19

*Wethersfiel*
*and*
*Ruislip*

**LEGAL**
**BRIEFIN**

Including notes on
NON-COOPERATION
POLICE & COURT PROCEDU
OBTAINING LEGAL ADVICE
OFFENCES & PENALTIES
YOUNG PERSONS & JUVENILE
OPEN PRISONS

---

### Public Assembly in Parliament Square, 29th April, 1961

This is a non-violent demonstration; please join it on this understanding. Do not be provoked to violence whatever the circumstances.

The police may try to stop the march down Whitehall. If they do demonstrators will sit down across the road until removed.

If the police arrest you or attempt to move you on, sit down, go limp and refuse to move until carried away.

As the road in Parliament Square will be occupied you may be arrested. Detailed General and Legal Briefings are being prepared by the Committee. Please fill in the coupon overleaf so that these can be sent to you.

CND Groups wishing to help — individuals for marshalling — offers for transport — requests for leaflets and posters should go directly to the Secretary, Committee of 100, 13 Goodwin Street, London, N.4. Telephone : ARChway 1239.

**COMMITTE**
**OF 100** ☮

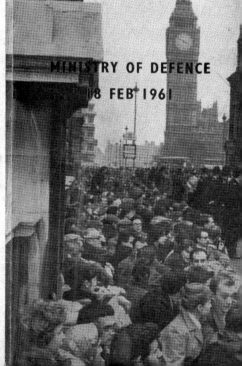

MINISTRY OF DEFENCE
18 FEB 1961

ll and Rev. Michael Scott in the non-violent demonstration outside the Ministry of Defence, ary, 1961.
Courtesy *Peace News*.

# ...ecause

Governments of East and West are
...pared to destroy mankind. War could start
...any moment. Today the crisis is Berlin.
...morrow it may be Laos, Congo, Formosa. With
...h new crisis the danger grows.
...anwhile the air is polluted by nuclear tests.

# war is inevitable

unless the people act to put an end to the
folly of the arms race.
The Government of Britain has refused to take
the lead. Now it is up to us—the
People of Britain—to act.

# ...eople of Britain resist!

## Saturday, 9th December 1961

### Details

The **Wethersfield** and **Ruislip** demonstrations are being organised
by the Committee of 100 in London. The demonstrations
in other areas are organised by the
local Committees.

### Wethersfield NATO Base

Coaches from Midland Road by St. Pancras Station 9.30 a.m.
March from Wetherfield Village 1 p.m.
Resistance at base : 1.15 p.m.—7 p.m.

The mass walk-on is an important operational air base
and the attempt to obstruct and reclaim it marks
a new phase in the development of resistance to nuclear
weapons. We need many thousands there
if it is to be effective. Please come to Wethersfield
if you possibly can.

### Ruislip U.S. Air Force Headquarters

Assemble : South Ruislip Underground Station 2 p.m.
(35 minutes from Holborn on the Central Line)
Resistance at base : 3 p.m.—9 p.m.

### Non-co-operation

As in previous demonstrations we urge those who are able
to do so to refuse bail, to refuse to pay fines and
refuse to be bound over, in order to make our resistance
more effective.

On this occasion, as a further step, we are calling
for 1,000 of our supporters to refuse to give their names and
addresses when arrested.

Members of Committee of 100—Earl Russell, O.M., F.R.S., President

Lady Clare Annesley
Margaretta Arden
Angela Aspinwall
Ernest Bader
Manny Blankett
E. J. Boothby
John Brailey
John Braine
Douglas Brewood, Senior
Douglas Brewood, Junior
Oliver Brown
David Broughton
Jane Buxton
Raymond Challinor
Terence Chandler
Howard Clewley
Mary Clark
Alan Cleary
Shelagh Delaney
Carol Fri-Gibbon
John Fri-Gibbon
J. Alun David
Elizabeth Dales
John Fletcher
Harrold Foster
William Gaskill
Janet Goodricke

Trevor Hatton
Dr. Franz Heymann
David Hoggett
Bill Holdsworth
Alac Horsley
Martin Hyman
Bill Kaye
Tom Kempinski
Rev. R. E. Kirkby
Ed. Lewis
Isobel Lindsay
Alan Lovell
Hugh MacDiarmid
George Melly
Peter McConardie
Dr. Jack Morgan
Dr. John Morris
R. E. Muirhead
John Nicholls
Michael Nolan
Pat O'Connell
P. O'Connor
Colin Painter
Rev. C. Palmer
Dr. Piper

Patrick Pottle
Eric Preston
Ines Randall
Mansell Randles
Sir Herbert Read
Mary Rexford
Vanessa Redgrave
Bruce Macgregor-Reid
Heather Richardson
Mary Ringsleben
Megsi Kosher
Chego Rosher
Edith Lady Russell
John Mush
Roger Michael Scott
Philip Seed
E. G. P. Rowe
Teddy Seruya
John Summerville
R.W. Smith
Peter Digby Smith
Tony Smythe
Anthony Southall
Mahala Trevaldwyn
Jon Tinker
William Warbis
Alex Wate

## ...OMMITTEE OF 100

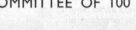

 ☮ mass resistance

will
you
take
part?

we
need
50,000

ndon, N.4

# WHY IN A

because the statement of East and West are prepared to go to war, nuclear war. They admit that millions would die. They know that there might be no survivors.

they admit that tests kill and are a danger to the health of future generations. Yet they are prepared to go on testing.

# DEMOCRACY

they know that war could come by accident. Several times already the bombers have been recalled only at the last moment. Leading scientists have warned that accidental war is not only possible but likely. But nothing is done. Rockets and bombers are on the alert. Continually.

# WE SIT DOWN

because this form of non-violent protest directly challenges the Government's preparations for war and expresses our determination to resist even at the risk of imprisonment.

in London at the centre of Government because it is the Government that plans war in our name.

at the bases because it is at these bases that the buttons will be pressed, the rockets fired, the bombers dispatched.

in the towns throughout the country because it is these towns that will be wrecked and burnt. We want their inhabitants to know the peril.

# WE RESIST

because we value freedom
democracy means nothing without freedom. This means above all freedom to live.

Hitler's slaughter of Jews could never have been democratic.

the preparations by Macmillan, Kennedy and Krushchev to kill millions of people can never be democratic.

the victims of nuclear war will not be consulted

because we have responsibility
the German people have been blamed for not resisting Hitler's policies

if we are to resist the policies of race, murder we must

# MASS
# RESISTANCE

Wethersfield
Ruislip
Brize Norton
York
Manchester
Bristol
Cardiff

### SATURDAY
### DECEMBER 9

Committee of 100

13 Goodwin Street
London, N.4.  ARC 1239

ANNOUNCES **SATURDAY** NON-VIOLENT CIVIL DISOBEDIENC

# 29

**A PUBLIC ASSEMBLY**

APRIL *in* **PARLIAMENT SQUARE**

☞ **gli office** 5 Caledonian Rd., N.1. 01-837 7174.

☞ **gay women** bookshop, gay commune. 01-624 1952

☞ **bethnal rouge** 248 Bethnal Green Rd E2. 01-739 1827

---

the Religious Gay Lib Group does exist.
meetings every fortnight
next meeting: Sunday 15th July, 2.30pm
18 Duncan Terrace, N.1.
phone 278 1701 for more details

**GAYSOC DANCE**

Friday 6th July, 8 - 1am
bareroupdisco
50p
Manning Hall, 1st floor, University of
London Union (ULU), Malet St, WC1.

In Aid of Gaysoc Bureaucracy.
Besides financing his struggle for power
Jamie Gardner tells they've also given
money to London GLF and Bethnal House.

**GAY MARXIST GROUP**

for information see Gay News.

**TRANSVESTITES & TRANSSEXUALS**
wanting to form group contact office.

**PIG OF THE WEEK award**

goes to Ilie 'Nasty' Nastase
Wimbledon tennis star, tipped to win the final;
Knocked out by an unknown American in the
first round.

People wanting to join
awareness groups
phone Brian 278 1701
who is co-ordinating this.

---

Sticker from the Icebreakers Group who can
give you some if you can use them.

┌─────────────────────────────────┐
│ Isolated homosexual men         │
│ and women can ring              │
│ Icebreakers on 01-274 9590      │
│ between 7.30 and 10.30          │
│ every evening of the year       │
│ to talk over their problems     │
│ with other Gay People           │
└─────────────────────────────────┘

**Brighton Gay Pride Week**

**BRIGHTON:** Sussex Gay Liberation Front
is staging Pride week, kicking off this
Tuesday July 3rd, with a meeting at the
Stanford Arms Hotel featuring Rose Robertson as guest speaker. Ms Robertson's counselling service to parents of gays has been
very much in the news of late.
On Friday, July 6th, the usual disco will
take place, with special prizes for the most
outrageous, and on Saturday a mature
drag show. On Saturday a Gay Pride march
will start at the Norfolk Square, Weston
Road, 1.30pm, finishing at the old fish-
market on the seafront. The same evening,
a dance will be held at the Royal Albion
Hotel opposite the Palace Pier. Admission
will be 40p.
Weather permitting, the week will wind
up on Sunday with a picnic on the beach
to the west of the Palace Pier.
- if you wish to know more, ring
Sussex GLF on 0273-683301.

---

**'I played like a
girl'**

---

# Gay Liberation Front
## Diary
### 4 - 10th JULY

**wednesday**
South London GLF  8pm
Oval House, near Oval tube

**thursday**
East London GLF, 103 Market St., E.6
West London GLF, Fulham Town Hall,
Fulham Broadway

**friday**
Brighton disco, Stanford Arms, Preston Circus.
Gaysoc dance : see back page

**saturday**
South London disco, 8pm Hanover Arms,
Clapham Rd, Oval tube
**BRIGHTON:** Gay Pride March 2.30
Norfolk Sq., Western Rd.
Dance, Royal Albion Hotel
opposite Palace Pier, 50p

**sunday**
picnic in Brighton, to west of
Palace Pier
Gay Day, Whitestone Pond, nr Jack Straws
Castle, Hampstead, 3pm
office collective 7pm
Gay Women's Group, Crown &
Woolpack, St John St, E.C.1.
Camden GLF 7.30. General
Picton, Caledonian Rd, N.1.

**monday**
West London disco 8pm
Fulham town Hall
All-London meeting 7.30
Conway Hall, Red Lion Sq,
Holborn tube.

**tuesday**

## JESUS FREAKS

These include many more people than just those who talk of the love of god. To me it's an attitude of mind that is found in the bible story itself. Jesus died on the cross so that we can find salvation. He had no self interest. He got no pleasure out of his pain. It was all done for the betterment of MAN.

The Altruism seems to me to be the way many politicos of the revolutionary left and the various christian and non christian do-gooders operate — we must do something for glf, we must help gay people; every-thing we do must be from motives other than those of self interest.

If christ had been leathery and colherne wise he would have enjoyed those moments on the cross and apart from that news of the sensation he would have lain forgotten. I will say he did enjoy it from the closet, like the school master who beats saying it hurts me more than you, like the cottage sex scene where you pretend to be peeing while having a wank. The world of scout masters & hairstylists, our world of good intentions & 'bad' thoughts. christ lived there.

Idealism from the closet, salvationism fed for world revolution, their sights riv-eted on landmarks as far removed from them-selves and their immediate needs as possible. The first rush of idealistic inspired energy may wither away like the first snow drops in spring, turning into cynics or un-touchable fanatics those particular occup-ants of the greater closet, ever reaching out for that invisible thing called revolut-ion.

Worse still christ was a man, little boys must be good father was a man, the closet trick sir, but of course they're not gods but sinners. Menwhile the blessed virgins, the feminine sex are fully employed mopping up the mess and mum, the queen of heaven, stuck up on her pedestal or tied to the home, is forever ir terceeding for us so that daddy in heaven doesn't punish us for our selfish naughtines The boys in glf decide that being themsel-ves (gay) is not sinful, sex is wonderful, we must tell everyone the good news. I want to help you, a new class of sexy saints has emerged.

They talk of how children should be looked after, but not for them the nappy changing, tething problems, accidents and the day to day word of the home, the man ruled by his head and the heads of others and if he has come out the mood of the moment, gets into helping humanity his sights levelled as far from himself as possible.

---

The saints often prefer to talk of people, not women, not homosexuals, not black etc always the oppression is universal coming from those at the top, never from themselves. Leafleting fleet st or even perhaps fight-ing wars under the sacred flag of glf will bring us together— and after that people drift back to their flats, bedsits, squats and communes, some speaking with the voice of thousands of pounds a year, some on £11 a week on social security, others working in hotels or offices earning £15 to £25 a week, all are brought together in their isolation from the familied rest but sep-arated from one another in their life styl

### WHAT GLF IS FOR ME.

glf is
 — living in communes
 — being responsible for each other
 — sharing responsibility for children
 — enjoying life together
 — growing old together
 — nudity, not hiding from each other
 — hate for the evils done to us
 — openly loving our friends
 — sharing our wealth.
 — lots of sex.

MICHAEL

### Unity and brotherliness in GLF

A thing that has been bothering me a lot recently is how little how few I feel in common with so few gay brothers in GLF. Indeed there seem to be quite few gay brothers who I dislike quite intensely because of the way they behave in and out of meetings and because of things they say.

I find this rather depressing because I know the I come to GLF because of my sense of loneliness, and because I need to meet other gay men and women. I think this must be true of most of us

I find more and more that the only people I feel I have something in common with are the people who've made the break with their past and live communally with other people. Although I have differences with many of the people living in communes these are the people I find myself feeling closest to. Other than that I seem to prefer the company of gay men who shun any kind of 'political' activity and have a healthy scepticism about the whole thing and get on with feeling closest to. Other than that I seem to all I like to get on with each other but we're ad equally certain that our own attitudes and idea the right ones. So there is a feeling of be betrayal when we fail to agree; we feel let down by people we expected to be our friends. We would stop talking and hostility builds up.

this explains, I think . why I am so passionate

---

straight journalists, the CHE executive seem much the same as any straight bureaucratic socia workers or 'community' workers, the academics from the LSE Gay Culture Society seem just as academic and aloof as any straight academic, and the gay icebreakers seem just as confused and confusing as any straight samaritan or do-gooder.

All these kinds of straight people - marxists, vicars, journalists, social workers, academics, and samaritans are the sort of people I can't stand - they all seem to be finding ways of avoiding being honest with themselves and with us. These sort of people are always oppressive to gay men and women. And I tend to dislike their gay counterparts as much as the straights themselves.

In fact, I am always much more conscious of my dislike for these gay do-gooders because some sense of involvement with them - we're all gay and we all say we're interested in getting a better life for gay men and women.

David McLellan

---

The Saga of a Non-entity called the GLF Office.

On Sunday 24th June the office collective decided after a lot of discussion to run the office until Tuesday 26th June when it would be put to the GLF general meeting that unless the meeting can implement a working office routine and form a new off-ice collective the office collective will resign from Tuesday morning and will not continue to function without a clear mandate to do so.

The meeting on Tuesday might decided noth-ing and did not implement anything that the off-ice collective needs a week and closed all day. The idea of the office collective deci-sion on Sunday was to get an office working properly with a group of people actually running it.

As Tuesdays meeting was not even interest-ed in running the office or some were prov-iding that they themselves did not have to run it, why should we bother with an office? and why is it open when we have no office co-collective to run it?

David McLellan

in my hostility towards some gay brothers, when I do wish we could all be friends - it's because we can only win by being together, so any betraya is very upsetting.

On the other hand, if I was cast away on a desert island with the editor of the Times and Dennis Lemon (editor of Gay News), I know who I'd spend my time with. I have met the Archbishop of Cant-erbury at a public meeting, so I know that Brian Burt is a million times nicer. If I were to meet Tariq Ali or Robin Blackburn I'd probably fall in love with Phil Powell by comparison. Tony Salvis must be much more lovable than Vic Feather, and Michel Feled-Plaechkens more than John Presshwater. Compared with Digby Jacks (president of the National Union of Students) Jamie Gardner might seem as far out as Mae West. And I set Sir William Armstrong (head of the Civil Service) has got nothing on Paul Temper-ton (Mr. William, M.M.) secretary of the CHE bureau-cracy.

But until these straight pigs actually do begin to threaten my life and well-being in a very drastic way, or until some of us begin to change. I'm afraid I'll continue to feel that these gay brothers have more in common with my enemies than they do with me, and I'll have to try and find my real friends where I can. (Bob)

# GLF.ST

# IF YOU DIG IT DO IT

The streets are yours.... make them sing....open out
People like people like you.... come to life.... why
make strangers when you could make friends.... react
respond.... we are now part of your life, become part
of ours....or his....or hers....or theirs....right now.
AND THINK
HOW CAN LOVE CORRUPT, WHEN

## there are as many sexes.... as there are people.

The G.L.F. is fighting for your freedom, as well as ours.
GAY LIBERATION COMES TOGETHER    AT 7.30 p.m. EACH WEDNESDAY AT
THE LONDON SCHOOL OF ECONOMICS
HOUGHTON STREET

# Gay Liberation diary

Apr 5–11

G.L.F 5 Caladonian Rd. N.1.

**Thursday 5th**
East London G.L.F.
103 Market St.
East Ham

Camden G.L.F
44 Parkhill Rd. N.W.3.

West London G.L.F.
Fulham Town Hall
Fulham Broadway

South London G.L.F.
Minet Library
Knatchbull Rd
Brixton

**Friday 6th**
Hitch to Morecambe

**Saturday 7th**
G.L.F Come Together in Morecambe
and
Psychologists Conspiracy in Liverpool

**Sunday 8th**
Same as Saturday

**Monday 9th**
South London Dis
St Matthews Crypt
Brixton 15p adm
Free Drin

GAY Womens GROUP
at Crown and WOOLPA
394 St. John St. E.C

**Tuesday 10th**
No west Londo
Disco.... Booo!

**Wednesday 11th.**
Fly to Rio
or Visit
or Bath
o

TEL. 837 7174

# vest london gay lib.

## free disco ☺

+++++++++++++++++++++++++++

WEDNESDAY 15th MARCH. 8 - 00 pm. to 11 - 00 pm.

WHITE LION P.H. ( Putney Bridge ) Upstairs Bar.

+++ +++ N E W M E M B E R S W E L C O M E +++ +++

Info: From Gay Liberation Front 5,Caledonian Road, N. 1. Tel: 837 - 7174

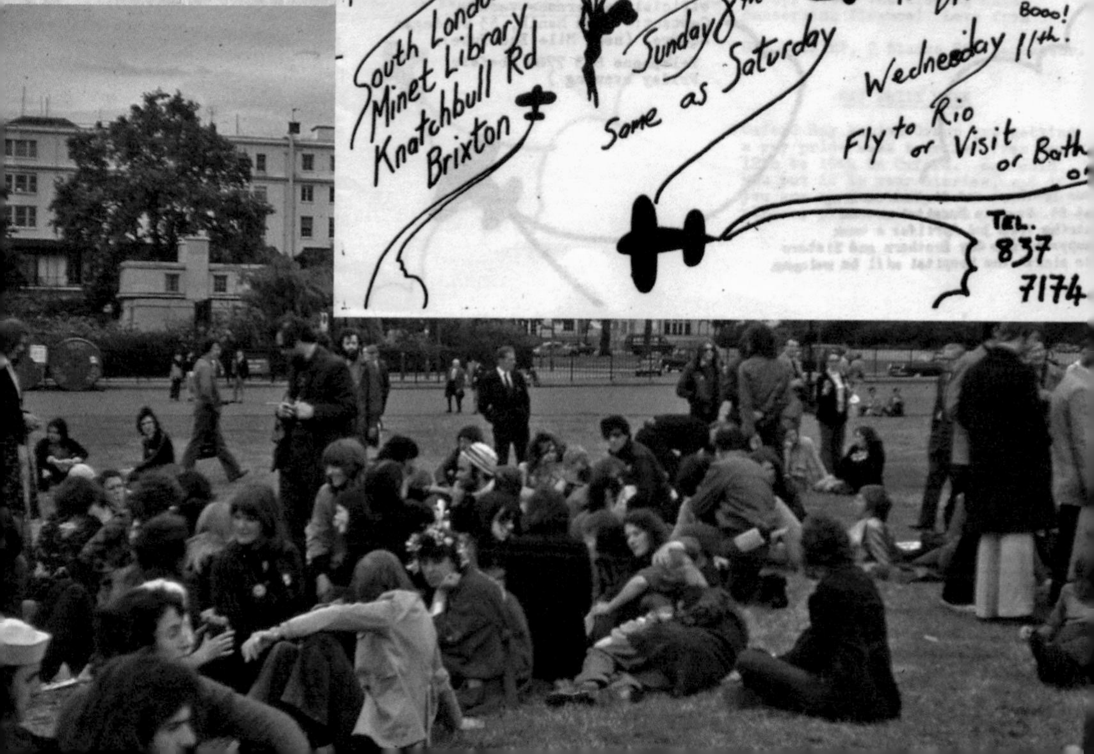

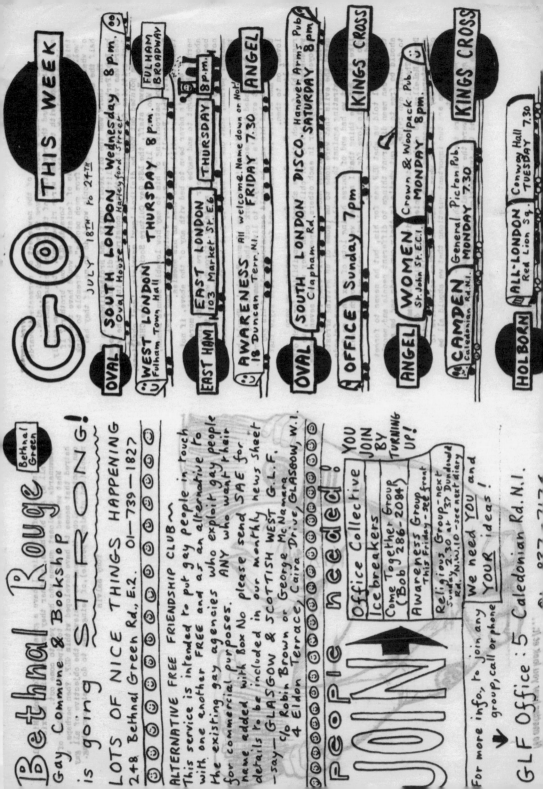

# GO THIS WEEK

JULY 18TH to 24TH

**OVAL** — SOUTH LONDON — Wednesday 8 p.m. — Oval House, Harleyford Street

FULHAM BROADWAY

**WEST LONDON** — THURSDAY 8 p.m. — Fulham Town Hall

**EAST HAM** — EAST LONDON — THURSDAY 8 p.m. — 103 Market St. E.6

ANGEL

**AWARENESS** — All welcome. Name down or Not! — FRIDAY 7.30 — 18 Duncan Terr. N.1

**OVAL** — SOUTH LONDON DISCO — Hanover Arms Pub, Clapham Rd. — SATURDAY 8 pm

**OFFICE** — Sunday 7 pm

KINGS CROSS

**ANGEL** — WOMEN — Crown & Woolpack Pub. — MONDAY 8 pm — St. John St. E.C.1

**CAMDEN** — General Picton Pub. — MONDAY 7.30 — Caledonian Rd. N.1

KINGS CROSS

**HOLBORN** — ALL-LONDON — Conway Hall, Red Lion Sq. — TUESDAY 7.30

---

# Bethnal Rouge
Bethnal Green

Gay Commune & Bookshop is going STRONG!

**LOTS OF NICE THINGS HAPPENING**
2+8 Bethnal Green Rd, E.2.  01-739-1827

**ALTERNATIVE FREE FRIENDSHIP CLUB**
This service is intended to put gay people in touch with one another FREE and as an alternative to the existing gay agencies who exploit gay people for commercial purposes. ANY who want their name added with Box No please send SAE for details to be included in our monthly news sheet —say— GLASGOW & SCOTTISH WEST G.L.F. c/o Robin Brown or George McNamara 4 Eldon Terrace, Caira Drive, GLASGOW, W.1.

## PEOPLE needed!
## JOIN

YOU JOIN BY TURNING UP!

Office Collective
Icebreakers
Come Together Group (Bob 286-2084)
Awareness Group — see front
This Friday — see front
Religious Group — next Sunday 2.30 at 37 Dunalsed Rd. N.W.10 — see next diary

We need YOU and YOUR ideas!

For more info, to join any group, call or phone

GLF Office: 5 Caledonian Rd. N.1.  01-837-7174

Why was the last issue of the newssheet so permeated towards many gay people that I love? Why was it so sick, sick, sick.
First we had the revelation of the office being vandalised and sabotaged with the phone wires ripped out, etc. Can we really call the people who act this way, towards GLF, our brothers? If this had been done by a group of facists, we would have thought, "Well, what can one expect from such people". I tremble to think of what the so-called gay people would do to me, if they had half the chance.

Then there was the bit about 'Unity and Brotherliness in GLF' by Bob. Perhaps he feels a little bitter and disillusioned, because there was very little, if anything, constructive, in what he wrote. Just criticism for criticism's sake.
He pointed out how he disliked 'gay' marriage, 'gay' christians, the 'Gay News' staff, the LSE Gay Culture Society and the CHE executive. Who does he like?
And how patronising of him to say how lovable Dennis Lemon, Brian Burt, Phil Powell, Tony Salvis, Jamie Gardner and Paul Temperton were, but still regard them as his enemies.
I bet he's never been to bed with any of the above, if not, perhaps he ought to and maybe he would find out a little more about them and they might appear a little more lovable to him, because although one can relate mentally, through sex, it is not complete until one has related physically, through sex, with another person, that one can begin to feel how the other person ticks.

Then there was Michael's piece on 'Jesus Freaks'. Should he not be reminded that people must work out their own life styles, as it is not everyone's life style to live in a commune or a squat. Perhaps if he had his way, he would concentrate all of his gay brothers and sisters into communes and force the life style that he loves, on to them.

I lived in the Pence Commune for seven months, we were responsible for each other, we shared responsibility for each other, we shared responsibility for children when they were there, we enjoyed life together in each others company, we grew seven months older together, we went around nude when we felt like it, we hated the evils that were done to us (some of us getting arrested for demonstrating against these evils), openly loving our friends, sharing what we had and of course having lots of sex when we felt like it. But one thing that I noticed was that although Michael, who proclaims his love for communal living, only visited us once, and that was when we gave a party.

Michael told us what GLF was for him, but he seems to forget that GLF can mean different things to different people and people should be free to work out what's in their own heads and be able to do their own thing.
The only person who bothered to give us his full name, was David McLellan, and although his piece was critical, he did pose some interesting questions, such as, Why should we bother with an office? or Why is it open when we have no office collective to run it? These are two important questions that we should all be thinking about.
But there were two things in the newsletter that made me feel good. These were the proposals to bring out another issue of "Come Together" and the information, about the "Icebreakers Group".
Does this mean a revival of the old spirit that first gave GLF its impetus.

In spite of all this, I have a great love for Bob, Michael, and all my gay brothers, whether they are christian, marxist, communard or closet queens who have yet to come out.
What we need is a bit more love to wipe out the canker of hatred that seems to have developed within GLF. Then perhaps we can continue along the road to achieving the objective of all gay people and straight people, of being free to do their own thing.

Tony Salvis

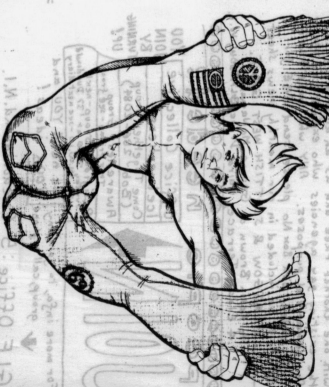

No matter how you look at it...

# COME TOGETHER

**AT THE GAY LIBERATION FRONT DANCE IN KENSINGTON TOWN HALL - YES KENSINGTON ON TUESDAY THE TWENTY-SECOND OF DECEMBER THERE'S A BAR EXTENSION - GROUPS & DISCOTEQUE THE TICKETS ARE ON SALE NOW - ONLY SIX SHILLINGS**

# COME OUT

**AGAINST - DISCRIMINATION AND OPPRESSION BY THE LAW - BY SOCIETY - AND BY EMPLOYERS FOR - REDUCING THE AGE LIMIT OF CONSENT TO THAT OF HETROSEXUALS - WHAT EVER THAT MAY BE AGAINST - PSYCHIATRY WHICH REGARDS US AS SICK**

# COME ALONG NOW

# DANCE

Gay Liberation Front

St PANCRAS TOWN HALL

FRI June 2nd 7.30-12.00

Goblin Monksilver Disco
Lightshow Bar

50p

# GAY WOMENS LIBERATION

SPECIAL CELEBRATION
WOMENS DISCO

ON INTERNATIONAL WOMENS DAY
10th MARCH, 1973.

AT THE CROWN WOOLPACK
St. JOHN ST. EC1.
(Nr. ANGEL TUBE)
8 P.M. — 12 P.M.

COME TOGETHER

15p.

The streets are yours.... make them sing....open out

make strength when you could make interest when

FAIR PLAY FOR GAY !

homosexuals claim the right to love

Did you wait till you were 21 ?

GLAD TO BE GAY

GAY LIBERATION FRONT

NO MORE SEX ROLES

GAY -BUT NOT ASHAMED

there are million gay in the world from people

SUSSEX GAY LIBERATION FRONT

there are as many sexes.... as there are people.

WHEN

respond.... we are now part of your life, become part

HOW CAN LOVE CORRUPT,

of ours....or his....or hers....or theirs....right now.

# CHAPTER 3

## JOLLY GOOD TENANTS

## Gay Liberation Front

In February 1971, while *Peace News* were already debating their departure, the Gay Liberation Front (GLF) arrived at 5 Cally Road and opened an office in a small room at the back of the basement, which had previously been let to London CND. Harry Mister remembered this as an important turning point for the building:

> We were flooded with hordes of extraordinary people, and they were jolly good tenants, they stayed a long time. In a way we had a minor part in the gay community coming out.[1]

The first Gay Liberation Front started in New York, after a police raid in 1969 on the Stonewall Inn was fiercely resisted by its customers. Images of the confrontation spread around the world. London GLF held its first meeting on 13 October 1970, inspired by two students, Aubrey Walter and Bob Mellors, who went to the Black Panther Party's Revolutionary People's Constitutional Convention in Philadelphia. The convention had gay liberation on its agenda after Huey Newton, a Black Panther leader, made a speech arguing for solidarity with gay people.

The early meetings of the GLF in London gathered gay people who were ready for radical change.[2] Some had been involved in other forms of activism before or been part of the growing counterculture, while others were new to radical politics. One early member, Stuart Feather, described his first GLF meeting:

> I joined the Gay Liberation Front on what I think was the third meeting that it had. Three friends of mine, my boyfriend and another gay couple, were out shopping one day in Oxford Street and had this leaflet thrust into their hand inviting people to come to a meeting of the Gay Liberation Front at the London School of Economics. So, they came back and told me about this. And I was immediately interested because I recalled that I had [read] ... about a Gay Liberation Front in New York, and I had wondered what on earth that could be. It was quite a puzzle to me. I mean I had heard of liberation fronts of Palestine and the Western Sahara, but the idea of a gay liberation front was just beyond me. I was very curious.
>
> We went along to the meeting ... I was then 30 years old, and I came into a meeting of about fifty gay men and lesbians, the like of which I had never seen before. I had never seen people like this in any of the pubs or clubs that I had been to. They were all students mainly, in their twenties, some the same age as me. And we were asked a question by one of the lesbians. She asked us to think about the way we behaved in order to disguise

1   'Interview with Harry Mister by Alan Dein for King's Cross Voices.

2   'Gay' is the term used and popularised by the Gay Liberation Front. It is used here in lieu of LGBTQ+ in

keeping with the language used at the time.

3   LSE Library, *Gay Liberation Front Demands*, 2017 <https://www.flickr.com/photos/lselibrary/36153317966/> [accessed 22 September 2022].

Brighton Pride, 1973

our sexuality at work. And I suddenly saw all the sort of games that I played flash before my eyes, and I was quite saddened and rather upset, that I was playing all these games, and it did seem to be deceitful. And I knew why I was playing them of course. And so, I could immediately see what they meant when they talked about oppression and the way we had adapted to it, or accepted it, and were behaving within permitted parameters, as far as they were tolerated. So, I was immediately involved.

A list of demands was written up and voted on at one of the early meetings. The demands included an end to all discrimination against gay people, 'male or female', that the age of consent be made the same as that for heterosexuals and that gay people be able to hold hands and kiss in public.[3]

# THE GAY LIBERATION FRONT DEMANDS....

- that all discrimination against gay people, male and female, by the law, by employers, and by society at large, should end

- That all people who feel attracted to a member of their own sex should know such feelings are good and right,

- That sex-education in schools stop being exclusively heterosexual

- That psychiatrists stop treating homosexuality as though it were a problem or a sickness, and thereby giving gay people senseless guilt complexes

- That gay people be as legally free to contact other gay people, through newspaper ads, on the streets, and by any other means they want, as are heterosexuals, and that police harassment should cease right now

- That employers should no longer be allowed to discriminate against anyone on account of their sexual preferences

- That the age of consent for gay men be reduced to the same age as for heterosexuals

- That gay people be free to kiss and hold hands in public, as are heterosexuals

## GAY IS GOOD!

## ALL POWER TO THE OPPRESSED PEOPLE

London GLF meetings: Wednesdays, 7.30
43 King St, WC2

office: 5, Caledonian Rd, N.1.

---

# THE GAY LIBERATION FRONT DEMANDS:

*that all discrimination against gay people, male and female, by the law, by employers, and by society at large, should end,

*that all people who feel attracted to a member of their own sex should know that such feelings are good and natural,

*that sex-education in schools stop being exclusively heterosexual,

*that psychiatrists stop treating homosexuality as though it were a problem or a sickness, and thereby giving gay people senseless guilt-complexes,

*that gay people be as legally free to contact other gay people, through newspaper ads, on the streets, and by any other means they want, as are heterosexuals, and that police harassment should cease right now,

*that employers should no longer be allowed to discriminate against anyone on account of their sexual preferences,

*that the age of consent for gay men be reduced to the same age as for heterosexuals,

*that gay people be free to hold hands and kiss in public, as are heterosexuals.

# ALL POWER TO
# OPPRESSED PEOPLE!

Just over a month after their first meeting, on 27 November 1970, the GLF organised the first public demonstration of gay people in Britain in protest at the arrest of Louis Eaks at Highbury Fields, Islington. Eaks, a prominent member of the Young Liberals, had been caught up in a police entrapment exercise and accused of 'indecency' with another man, although he insisted he had just been trying to get a light for his cigarette. The demonstrators gathered on Highbury Fields, held candles, lit each other's cigarettes and kissed each other openly.

In August 1971 the GLF Youth Group organised a march from a 'Gay Day' in Hyde Park to Trafalgar Square, where they held speeches calling for the age of consent to be lowered from 21 (for homosexual sex) to 16 (as it was for heterosexual sex.) Nettie Pollard remembered how liberating it was to march through the streets of London on that day:

> We had a march right through London, and up to Trafalgar Square. And everyone from GLF went, the older people as well. And there were hundreds of people there, and also hundreds of police, not the nice friendly police that you might see these days, but people who looked pretty hostile, and there were nearly as many police as there were demonstrators ...
>
> There was a great deal of solidarity, people were marching down the road on the way, and we were chanting, we had Gay Liberation Front banners, and women and men were marching arm-in-arm ... and kissing as we went, some of us. And the onlookers, even tourists, were looking totally mystified by it. I think most of them had no idea what the word 'gay' meant. Because you wouldn't believe that now, but people didn't know what gay meant, quite often. They might know what queer meant, or homosexual, but they were still unfamiliar with gay. Which is partly why we used it, it actually forged something of our own. So, it was a really joyous demonstration ... In the UK there had never been a [march] with LGBTQ+ people, actually out and proud and marching as if they have a right to exist. And some of the chants were, 'Give us a G.' 'G.' 'Give us an A.' 'A.' 'Give us a Y.' 'Y.' 'What does that spell?' 'Gay!' 'And what is gay?' 'Good.' 'What is gay also?' 'Angry.'

Gay Liberation Front Demands

In the space of just a few years, the GLF's inventive activism would make gay people visible in ways they had never been before. They held 'gay days' in parks, 'zapped' the Christian Festival of Light with theatrical direct action, supported feminist protests against the Miss World pageant and formed gay contingents on protests against the Industrial Relations Bill, the war in Vietnam and British troops in Northern Ireland. John Lloyd, then a member of both the GLF and the Communist Party, said the GLF:

> changed politics brilliantly. It introduced music into protest, it introduced dance into protest. It influenced the whole radical movement for years to come, all radical movements. It was a party.

### The Office

One of Housman's workers, Max McLellan (also known as David), was a member of the GLF and it is likely he suggested they move into the basement room at 5 Cally Road.

Stuart Feather described the office:

You went along this passage, quite a long passage, and then down the stairs to the basement. And there you were confronted by Dexion racks full of *Peace News*, and often you would see Pat Arrowsmith there rummaging through them, obviously looking for past articles and stuff she wanted a quote from. And right at the back [was the office]. I don't think it was more than about eight foot wide, and it might have been ten or eleven feet long. It was kind of coffin-shaped if you like....

I recall the rent as being about £5 a week for this tiny little room. You couldn't swing a cat in it. I think [the] maximum it could hold [was] about eight people ... there was hardly room to move for the chairs, and the one desk that was acquired. But I worked at that time in an employment agency of all things, which I was managing, and previous to that I had worked in travel agencies, I knew all about office routines and everything to do with running an office, so I thought I could also work in the GLF office.

Julian Hows joined the GLF while still at school. He was a 'working-class boy' who identified as an anarcho-communist but found the left 'so boring'. At sixteen he helped to organise a school student strike at his school in South London and was arrested on a march to Lambeth County Hall. When 'a bunch of radical drag queens' from GLF moved into a commune next to Julian's school and were attacked by his fellow school students, he helped GLF members hand out leaflets in the school playground. He was eventually thrown out of school for being a 'corrupting influence'. He remembers going to the GLF office at 5 Cally Road along with some others from the GLF Youth Group:

I just hung out in that space. There was one phone. I'm sure that people ... were doing very important work. We were hanging out being kids, being teens. And you've got to remember [this was] pre-Internet, pre-mobile phone. At that point, the GLF phone was a pay phone on the wall. But people used to phone up, and if nobody else was around, we'd pick it up. 'Is that GLF?' 'Yes it is. Who are you? Where are you from? Why don't you come down here? We're having a really nice time here.' A bunch of crazy fifteen-, sixteen- and seventeen-year-olds and [older] people like Cloud [Downey] used to say, 'Oh, come on, you know, be serious, give the phone to me.'

The office was a meeting place, somewhere to receive enquiries and correspondence and a place people could stop by, although it was so small not many people could squeeze in. People would drop in, as Julian did, or call up looking for help and support. Stuart Feather said 'it was a bit like a social centre':

We had to deal with lots of young male prostitutes who were hanging around King's Cross and Euston station and discovered the GLF office and they would come and bend our ears for a while on what they were doing, and why, and so on. And they'd all be made a cup of tea or a cup of coffee, and one would spend some time listening to their stories. And these kids were homeless as well. And then there were homeless gay men, and perhaps some lesbians. We began to run crash pads, so if people came up to London, escaping from their families and so forth, they could stay for a short while in one of our crash pads, and then probably move to another one, and eventually get on their own two feet. So, that was part of the work in the office.

And the telephone would be ringing frequently, people either ringing to know if we really existed, and for some sort of reassurance, or [for] help, or in a bad way. I remember one evening receiving a phone call from a transsexual who was living in a council hostel in Harlesden, who was completely freaked out.[4] And, so the two of us in the office ... decided ... to go out there, to see this person. And we did, and arranged a crash pad for her, and she decided to leave the hostel, and move into a crash pad. And that was Claudia, who was the first transsexual who joined the Gay Liberation Front.

Like the other areas of work in GLF, the office had its own 'collective' or working group. Stuart Feather explained that one of the 'very few rules in GLF' was that you could only join the office collective for three months, after which you had to take a break. As a focus point for an otherwise decentralised organisation, the office was both useful and a potential problem, as Stuart Feather described:

I was already conscious of the way bureaucracies can so easily build up, and people came along who were there for some purposes of their own, like advancing their career, or some such nonsense. And, as I worked there in the office, I could see that this kind of attitude could develop. And indeed, it did in the end.

John Lloyd joined the office collective in 1973. He remembers 'the core activity was the phone', with some getting in touch for basic support, others with serious legal cases. He helped build up a network of lawyers who could help people arrested for soliciting or 'indecency'. He remembers there being different approaches about 'how to handle people' who contacted the office. Some GLF members would 'challenge' people, he explains, to 'try ... to get people to change their lifestyle, and then therefore change themselves'.

Nettie Pollard was not part of the office collective, but remembers writing a challenging response to a research enquiry when she stopped by the office one day:

---

4    The use of 'transsexual' here instead of trans or transgender
     reflects the language that was used at the time.

I remember there was a letter from a student saying … 'I'm doing a project. Please tell me about male homosexuality.' And so, we wrote back (and I thought, I'm only doing this because it's GLF) … saying, 'You should be writing [about] your own oppression,' and sending her lots of information about lesbianism. So, if [we'd been part of the] Campaign for Homosexual Equality, which wanted equal laws, then obviously we would have sent her something on male homosexuality. I sort of felt a little bit guilty about it, like we hadn't really helped her, but on the other hand, maybe we made her think a little bit.

Between the summer of 1971 and the summer of 1972, three major disagreements developed within GLF. First, an argument about whether socialism or sexuality should take priority. Second, many of the women split away to form their own group due to sexism they experienced from the men. Then, another split emerged, between the radical feminist men or 'queens' who dressed in drag and often lived together in communes and the 'civil rights' activists or 'straight gays' as the radical queens called them.[5]

Stuart Feather, one of the 'queens', described how he saw the dispute:

The problem was between the men and the women really in Gay Liberation; the women were becoming more feminist, and the men were not interested; they were not interested in questioning their own femininity, their own male chauvinism, their own misogyny. They completely didn't want to know about those issues. They were men who didn't want to question themselves, really. And so, we who were sort of on the feminine side anyway, and pro women, pro feminism, we termed all those men the straight gays, and of course the office being sort of bureaucratic and everything, and so suited to men's traditional behaviour, began to fill up and be dominated by straight gays. And in the end, they were even not disclosing where their once-a-week office collective meeting took place.

The week before the first Pride march in July 1972, which was organised by GLF, there were a series of arguments in the office. First, the radical queens painted the office in bright colours, only to find that the office collective had repainted it in more conservative tones just a few days later.[6] As the first Pride march was being organised, the two groups argued, and the queens were accused of throwing the others out of the office for refusing to wear dresses.

In 1973 some of the 'radical queens', including Stuart Feather and Julian Hows, were living in a commune in the former radical bookshop, Agitprop, in Bethnal Green, East London. When Agitprop closed, the queens took over the lease and the

5   Lisa Power, No Bath but Plenty of Bubbles: An Oral History of the Gay Liberation Front, 1970–1973 (London: Cassell, 1995), p. 248.

6   Power.

7   Stuart Feather, Blowing the Lid: Gay Liberation, Sexual Revolution and Radical Queens (Winchester, UK; Washington, USA: Zero Books, 2015).

e are lesbians
--- and we are beautiful --

## Gay Liberation Front

The Gateways has made thousands of pounds out of women who come to the club (precisely how much money and publicity was gained from "The Killing of Sister George"?) yet the management of the Gateways considers Lesbians to be sick

We are not sick and don't like people who condescendingly treat us as such - especially when they are making a living off us --

Gay is Good --
Come to the

## Gay Liberation Front People's Dance

# GAY IS GOOD

Gay Liberation Front
GENERAL LONDON MEETING
Conway Hall, Red Lion Square, WC1
Every Tues at 7.30 beginning 29 May

Local meetings in South, East and West London and Camden - 837 7174 for information
Women's meetings 839 3918

GLF leaflets

bookshop, renaming it Bethnal Rouge. At an all-London meeting in October 1973, Stuart Feather proposed that the GLF office should move to Bethnal Rouge: there was plenty of space for it there and it would take the office away from the control of the 'straight gays'.[7] The proposal was discussed in the meeting but not voted on. Stuart Feather described what happened next:

> I did do something about it which was very unpopular and was probably wrong of me to do it, but nevertheless, I thought the only solution for the office was for us to go in there and remove all the office papers and take them to our commune in Bethnal Green, Bethnal Rouge. And that is what we did, and that caused a huge furore.

Early on 3 October, the day after the meeting, Stuart drove a group over to Caledonian Road in his van. They rushed in, seized what paperwork they could grab and took it back to Bethnal Rouge.

Despite the queens' raid, an office at Bethnal Rouge was never fully established, and the office collective continued at 5 Cally Road. A communique from

london 1971                              10p

*gay*

*liberation*

*front*

# manifesto

the office collective to the rest of GLF asked for the groups around the country to pay a regular subscription to keep it 'providing a valuable service from the most famous gay address in the world'.[8]

The London-wide GLF meetings ended in January 1974, and although many local groups in London and around the country continued, the most active years of the GLF had passed. The GLF office collective called a crisis meeting at 5 Cally Road to consider its future. Around 30 people came and decided to set up a helpline for the many callers who contacted the GLF office. The new 'London Gay Switchboard' would be run by people from GLF, along with gay organisations like Friend, Albany Trust and the Campaign for Homosexual Equality. It would use the GLF office and phone number. After placing a small advert in *Gay News*, London Gay Switchboard took its first call in March 1974. Forty-five people rang in the first five hours.[9] By the next year the switchboard was taking calls 24 hours a day, seven days a week. It would stay at 5 Cally Road until 1993 (see Chapter 5 for more on Switchboard.)

Switchboard, or London Gay Switchboard as it was known then, was one of the most successful of the many groups to grow, directly or indirectly, from GLF. In her oral history of the GLF, Lisa Power likened the movement to a dandelion, that flowered and then turned into a head of seeds that blew away to start new plants.[10]

A few people from the GLF office collective, including Housmans worker Max (David) McLellan, formed the GLF Information Service to sell GLF merchandise like badges and the manifesto from 5 Cally Road. A communique written on 12 March 1975, 'Where, What and Why is GLF at no.5 the Cally!?', explained 'we see ourselves as a clearing house for GLF'.[11] Profits from the sale of merchandise, including 'Glad to be Gay' and 'Avenge Oscar Wilde' badges went towards the discos organised by John Lloyd and others at the Prince Albert pub close to Caledonian Road (now the long running LGBTQ+ venue Central Station). When the GLF Manifesto was sold out, the GLF Information Service reprinted it — but controversially removed a section on communes they did not agree with. The GLF Information Service remained at 5 Cally Road until 1996.[12]

8   'Letter from GLF Office Collective, Undated', Bishopsgate Institute, David 'Max' McLellan Archive.

9   'The Story behind the UK's Biggest LGBTQ+ Helpline', *Huck Magazine*, 2019 <https://www.huckmag.com/perspectives/activism-2/switchboard-the-story-behind-the-uks-biggest-lgbtq-helpline/> [accessed 21 May 2022].

10   Power.

11   Gay Liberation Front, 'Where, What and Why Is GLF at No. 5 the Cally!?', 12 March 1975, Bishopsgate Institute, David 'Max' McLellan Archive.

12   Feather.

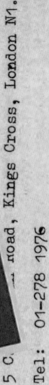

5 C. ...road, Kings Cross, London N1.

Tel: 01-278 1976

Wednesday, 20 November 1974

# HYPOCRISY!

**CAMPAIGN AGAINST ARMS TRADE**

## While we speak of peace

# CHAPTER 4

# NOT SO PEACEFUL IN KING'S CROSS

/e ▋▋ I a ms

After *Peace News* decamped for Nottingham in 1974, those left behind in 5 Cally Road barely had time to draw breath before the building was called on to provide sanctuary to an escaped fugitive, subjected to a police raid, the scene of a terrorist bombing and embroiled in a political trial.

At this time of seemingly relentless challenges, the space that *Peace News* had vacated in the building was put to good use. Two of the major political trials of the period, one involving the British Withdrawal from Northern Ireland Campaign (BWNIC) and the other the 'ABC trial', both used 5 Cally Road for their defence campaigns. The other rooms were used by the London Gay Switchboard, who moved out of the basement to lighter and brighter (but still quite cramped) rooms upstairs, Pax Christi, a Catholic peace organisation who opened an office in 5 Cally Road in 1972, the Middle East Research and Action Group, Radical Research Publications and Campaign Against Arms Trade (CAAT).

## A Bomb Blast

Campaign Against Arms Trade (CAAT) was launched by a coalition of peace, development and other organisations in 1974 and was based at 5 Cally Road until 1986. Valerie Flessati, who worked at Pax Christi at the time, described how CAAT began:

> There was a steering committee drawn from different organisations and supporters. I think [it's] been an enormously successful organisation, and it began really because in the early seventies there was a movement called Direct Action Training, and at that point nobody was quite clear what we would be training for, and so there was a big discussion with representatives of different peace organisations saying, well what's a common issue that we all want to work on, or are working on, that might need nonviolent action? And the arms trade was the common issue. So that's how that organisation came into being. It was really a communal thought process by different peace organisations.

CAAT started with a bang, quite literally, when its first ever mailing to supporters was inadvertently blown up by the IRA. Albert Beale, who had stayed behind in London when *Peace News* left for Nottingham, was the first person to work for the new campaign. On 25 November 1974, Albert had just finished painstakingly preparing CAAT's first ever newsletter to its supporters:

> This is in the days of typing on a stencil and hand-cranking [a duplicator] and running off sheets of paper … and the smell of correcting fluid that you'd use to take out things on the stencil that you'd cut by mistake. Anyway, so did the first of those newsletters … put them all in envelopes, got them all ready to roll and in those days we had a pillar box outside

Campaign Against Arms Trade leaflet, 1978 about the UN Special Session on Disarmament and the British Army Equipment Exhibition

While we speak of peace
We sell arms

**United Nations Special Session on Disarmament**

New York, 23 May–28 June 1978

**British Army Equipment Exhibition**

Aldershot, 19–23 June 1978

for further information:

**CAMPAIGN AGAINST ARMS TRADE**　5 Caledonian Road London N1 tel 01-278 1976

# HYPOCRISY!

Britain already sells more than £1000 million worth of arms per year. But it wants to sell even more, and so every two years the Defence Sales Organisation—part of the Ministry of Defence—runs the "British Army Equipment Exhibition" at Aldershot.

This year, the Aldershot arms fair is being held from 19–23 June. It thus coincides with the first-ever United Nations Special Session on Disarmament, taking place from 23 May–28 June. The timing well illustrates the hypocrisy of a government which says it wants peace but at the same time actively promotes the sale of weapons which can only be used for war.

The Aldershot exhibition is open only to overseas customers, not to the British public. In 1976, military representatives from 58 countries viewed the wares of 125 British companies, many of them household names like EMI and British Leyland. This year more than 200 companies are taking part in the exhibition, and there will almost certainly be more customers as well.

Britain has submitted a draft programme of action on disarmament to the U.N. Special Session. It says that U.N. member states should "seek to restrain the world-wide build-up of conventional weapons". A high-level British team, including the Prime Minister and the Foreign Secretary, is attending the Special Session, urging adoption of this programme of action.

And at the same time, a high-level team from the Ministry of Defence is selling arms at Aldershot.

\*　　\*

The Campaign Against Arms Trade opposes the British Army Equipment Exhibition at Aldershot, and all other attempts to sell British arms abroad. The Campaign encourages conversion of military industry to peaceful, socially useful production.

For more information about the Campaign, please send this form to CAAT, 5 Caledonian Road, London N1 9DX, tel 01-278 1976.

Please send me information about CAAT.

NAME

ADDRESS

PHONE

**CAMPAIGN
AGAINST
ARMS
TRADE**

number 5 ... I went out at the end of the afternoon with the first CAAT mailing and shoved them all in the letter box outside. [Then] I trotted off up to Euston to go to ... the PPU headquarters [for a meeting].

**Diana Shelley and bookshop worker Jim Huggon were talking in the basement when they heard a loud bang. Diana remembered:**

I thought, oh God, somebody's knocked over a bookshelf. I was very used to explosions, having spent the summer in Belfast, but it's totally different if you're underground. Because what you're feeling even at a very long distance, is the shockwave of the air on an explosion, as well as the bang. And underground, you didn't get any of [that] ... So, it was a little while before I think anyone came and told Jim and me that there had just been an explosion outside ... a couple of people were hurt, but not terribly seriously.

**Not long after Albert reached the PPU offices up the road in Euston, the bombing of a 'peace movement building' in central London came on the news:**

And then I thought, 'Well, bloody hell, there aren't many peace movement buildings in central London, so I abandoned the meeting I was at and ran all the way back to Cally Road. And as I turned the corner I hit some police tape, and there indeed was Cally Road taped off by the police. It ... was dusk by then, lights in the dark, and with the backdrop of the big *Peace News* sign on the front of the building, stretching massive letters across on the building; below this sign was a rather blown-up post box. The big heavy circular lid had blown straight up in the air and come down and landed on the old Volvo estate car owned by Harry Mister, who ... used it for deliveries and things, and rather dented the roof of his jalopy. And the post box itself was a bit asunder. And blowing up and down the gutter were all these bits of CAAT newsletter. And the envelopes. Which I was a bit cheesed off about ... it just seemed the opposite of poetic justice somehow ...

I mean it was the IRA bombings which were the news, the media didn't care much that it was the CAAT newsletter. Although, the back page of the *Guardian* next morning had a picture of ... this kind of slightly askew *PN* sign swinging in the breeze in the streetlights with some sort of witty *Guardian* [headline], 'Not So Peaceful in King's Cross Last Night'.

The IRA had not targeted 5 Cally Road in particular, it was simply the closest post box they could find to King's Cross Station. Adding to the ironic nature of this incident was that by this point, Albert was one of a group of people facing serious criminal charges for campaigning with the British Withdrawal from Northern Ireland Campaign (BWNIC).

1    '18 Months for Leafletting Soldiers', *Peace News*, 24 May 1974.

# Pat picked up at 'PN'

*Peace News'* London office became a rather insecure sanctuary for Pat Arrowsmith on Saturday evening, September 7. Pat, who was imprisoned in May under the Incitement to Disaffection Act, escaped from Askham Grange "open" prison 13 days earlier as part of her policy of non-co-operation with her imprisonment.

She decided to address the anti-National Front rally and was promised that she could speak from the official platform of the Amalgamated Union of Engineering Workers, only to be told at the last minute that she couldn't. So Pat spoke from the International Marxist Group platform. Police made just one attempt to breach the protective lines formed in front of the IMG platform, but withdrew after fights with these grim-faced and hard-hatted guardians.

After the rally, Pat asked for sanctuary at the National Council for Civil Liberties, but was turned away. So she came to *Peace News'* London office. From here she phoned the press who, in turn, phoned the police, it seems. Soon police appeared on the doorstep to say they'd heard rumours that Pat was in the building. There followed an embarrassing 15-minute performance as the Superintendant asked if he could be treated as an individual and be allowed to have just a look around. Only if he took off his uniform and came in as a civilian, we said,. If he wanted to look around as a policeman, he would have to get a warrant. It got complicated when we were asked to see if Pat, who we were not prepared to admit was in the building , would like to talk to the police.

Next to arrive was Commander Lowndes of N division, who also asked if he could come in to talk with Pat. He got the same reply, at which point the superintendant waves his warrant like a flag, rallied his troops and charged into the building.

After an initial moment of nastiness, in which the *Peace News'* London worker was told he would be arrested, Pat was delicately extricated from the linked arms of about 15 supporters (all singing "We shall not be moved"), carried over their heads and out to a waiting police car. Although the situation got rather heated, the arrest was carried out with the minimum of force and no other arrests were made.

*Peace News* gave sanctuary to Pat, as it would give sanctuary to anybody who asked for it. But Pat was not, in fact, asking for sanctuary but for a public place to be arrested in. This fits in with her strategy of gaining maximum publicity in the hope that it will encourage more people to leaflet troops and bring more attention to the iniquities of the Incitement to Disaffection Act. She could be more sensitive towards the people whose help she asks, particularly with regard to security. Word got around that she was to attend the rally, and not just amongst nonviolent activists — some of whom were approached to surround her on the march in order to keep the police at bay. People who'd helped Pat were disconcerted to find after the rally that that morning's *The Times* had been able to predict that she would speak there.

## An Escaped Fugitive

The British Withdrawal from Northern Ireland Campaign (BWNIC) was launched in 1973 to demand the withdrawal of British troops from Northern Ireland so that a political solution to the conflict could be found by the Irish people themselves. As a pacifist campaign they did not support the armed struggle of either side, unlike the larger Troops Out Movement, who did not condemn armed struggle in support of the Republican cause.

BWNIC produced a leaflet to tell British soldiers about ways they could avoid fighting in Northern Ireland. Pat Arrowsmith, who had organised the Aldermaston march in 1958 and had remained an important figure in the peace movement since, was arrested for handing it out on a military base. On 20 May 1974, she was found guilty of incitement to disaffection for distributing the leaflets to soldiers and sentenced to eighteen months in prison.

In an article published in *Peace News* a few days later BWNIC made it clear they would not be deterred from continuing to leaflet British troops.[1] Meanwhile, Pat Arrowsmith was transferred to Askham Grange Open Prison, from which she promptly absconded. She re-emerged at a large antifascist demonstration in Hyde Park, where she hoped to be publicly rearrested as a publicity stunt for the campaign.

Nettie Pollard, who had been in the GLF and by 1974 was working for the National Council for Civil Liberties (NCCL), was at the demonstration that day. As a teenager in Youth CND, Pat Arrowsmith and her partner Wendy Butlin had been the only lesbians Nettie had ever heard of. She remembered what happened when Pat got up on a platform to speak:

She made a rousing speech, and then she looked round, she wasn't arrested. She'd expected of course to be arrested immediately. But wasn't. So, she came down, and 'Well what shall we do now?' And so, the lesbian and gay part of the crowd said, 'Right, well, come with us then.' I can't remember whether I said or she said about trying to get sanctuary at National Council for Civil Liberties, who were [in the office] even though it was Saturday, because they were doing sort of legal service for anyone that might have been arrested ... And so anyhow, we all got on the train, maybe nine, twelve of us, something like that, a mixture of women and men. And went up to the front door, and there was Henry Hodge, who was the chair of the executive committee [of NCCL] and was also a solicitor who would have been doing this legal work there. And he just said to me, 'You're not bringing Pat in here, Nettie!' Just exactly like that. And he shut the door.

So, 'Oh, what *are* we going to do?' Oh, right, okay, rejected, thank you very much. And then I think it was Pat said, 'Well, why don't we go to Housmans, to *Peace News*?' Oh. Off we went to Housmans, who of course were delighted to see us all. And we went up the back stairs ... and we walked all the way up to the very top floor. And there was a big room there that was fairly empty. And we thought, right, what are going to do now? But she still hadn't been arrested. So, we thought, I know what we'll do. We'll ring the *Daily Telegraph*. So, we rang the *Daily Telegraph*, and said there's a fugitive at Housmans Bookshop, 5 Caledonian Road. And so eventually, up turns the *Daily Telegraph*, and had a talk to us, and took photographs, and there was a photograph of us all on the front page of Sunday's *Telegraph* that week. And, in no time the police turned up. I think the *Telegraph* must have rung them. About five or six officers turned up. So, we started chanting and making speeches. And obviously they tried to get Pat, who sat on the floor, or lay on the floor, and what we did was hold on to her, hold on to a leg, hold on to an arm. Just held on to her, several of us. And so, the police were dragging us off her. And the moment that they dragged one of us off, another person stepped up and got hold of her. And so, we had this tussle for quite a long time. I mean we knew we weren't going to win; we were making a point; we were making a demonstration. And, so, eventually, they managed to get her. Of course, she refused to walk down, so they had to carry her down all three flights of stairs, which was quite amusing.

The next issue of *Peace News* voiced a mild complaint at 5 Cally Road being used in this way:

*Peace News* gave sanctuary to Pat, as it would give sanctuary to anybody who asked for it. But Pat was not, in fact, asking for sanctuary but for a public place to be arrested in. This fits with her strategy of gaining maximum publicity in the hope that it will encourage more people to leaflet troops and bring more attention to the iniquities of the Incitement to Disaffection Act. She could be more sensitive to the people whose help she asks, particularly with regard to security.[2]

## BWNIC on Trial

Early on 10 September 1974, just three days after Pat was rearrested in 5 Cally Road, Albert Beale woke in his home in north London to find several police officers standing at the end of his bed. Later the same day, around ten police officers raided 5 Cally Road and took the *Peace News*' London worker, John Hyatt, to Kings Cross police station for questioning. Simultaneous dawn raids took place all over the country to arrest other BWNIC members.[3]

These arrests, Albert reflected, put *Peace News* 'in the thick of a struggle' to support the arrested members of BWNIC, many of whom were also involved in the paper or with 5 Cally Road. They were charged with *conspiring* to contravene the Incitement to Disaffection Act, which meant they faced much longer prison sentences than if they had been charged with incitement to disaffection (the offence for which Pat Arrowsmith had already been sent to prison). It took over a year for the trial to come to court.

Albert remembered:

It wasn't nice having it hanging over you [all] that time. I mean I'd never been arrested for any minor offences. I'd had a few tangles with the police, but I'd never got as far as being arrested for anything in the past ... so I didn't manage to work my way up to it gradually via a few offences in magistrates' courts, it was straight into the Old Bailey, which meant that having lived through that I've been a bit blasé about legal things ever since.

In September 1975 the BWNIC trial began. It would sit for 51 days. Diana Shelley, who had recently been appointed as *Peace News*' London-based worker got down to work reporting on the trial and also acted as press officer for the defence campaign. She remembered her work at the time:

One, there was all the defence campaign that you had to do anyway. Two, there was actually reporting. And three, there was writing press releases, as often as there was anything to report, which could be almost every day sometimes. So, I had a very long working day. I'd do my stint in the Old Bailey, and then I'd come back to 5 Cally Road and start battering out press releases. And the wonderful Julia would photocopy them, and then, get on her bike and drop them round Fleet Street. And we got some good coverage actually ...

On 10 December, which is Human Rights Day, they were acquitted. Gwyn and John, who had already pleaded guilty ... got fined. But, all the charges of conspiracy were thrown out, and ... Well, that was another magic moment really. Quite amazing that ...

---

2   'Pat Picked up at "PN"', *Peace News*, 20 September 1974, p. 3.

3   'London Anti Militarists Raided', *Peace News*, 20 September 1974.

# DEFEND FREE SPEECH

# DEFEND THE 14! DROP THE CHARGES!

**14 PACIFISTS, who want to stop the war in Ireland, have been charged with conspiracy and face possible life imprisonment.**

## IF YOU CARE, CONTACT

The British Withdrawal From Northern Ireland Campaign Defence Group

Box 69 % 197 Kings Cross Rd. London W.C.1

∘ 01 837 9794 ∘

TRIAL OLD BAILEY - SEPT 29 FOR 6 WEEKS

To work so bloody hard and then to actually win, is always just amazing, rather than just working bloody hard and then not winning. I mean, as the jury came back and they answered each, 'What do you say to charge blah blah blah?', and [the foreman said], 'Not guilty', 'Not guilty,' 'Not guilty', 'Not guilty.' And I suddenly was aware of this peculiar sound of sort of sobbing, and realised it was me. Sat in the courtroom going, [sobbing sounds]. And it was just incredible.

**The long, stressful trial must have taken a toll on the personal lives of the defendants, many of whom, Albert said, expected to serve prison sentences. It also sapped the energy of the campaign, as Albert reflected:**

Inevitably if you're part of a campaign and half the campaign is about to be locked up, you knuckle down over that, and so the campaign really lost momentum. So, the authorities did succeed in taking a lot of the wind out of our sails as a campaign, even though they didn't get us locked up.

### ABC Defence Campaign

The BWNIC trial was not the only legal battle in which the building was involved. In December 1974 Housmans refused, despite the threat of legal action, to hand over copies of a pamphlet written by Radical Research Publications, who had recently opened an office in the building. The pamphlet described the influence of the CIA on members of the Labour Government, based on research undertaken for the *Sunday Times* magazine, which the paper had then decided not to publish. The *Sunday Times* took legal action against Radical Research Publications and Housmans, claiming the pamphlet's design was similar to their magazine. In the end, the court decided the pamphlet could remain on sale with the cover obscured. Minutes of a Housmans board meeting concluded 'some useful press publicity resulted from the action'.[4]

In 1977, the building became involved in another long trial, when it provided space for the ABC defence campaign. In 1976 *Time Out* had published an article, 'The Eavesdroppers', about the previously unknown Government Communications Headquarters (GCHQ). The article was written by freelance journalist Duncan Campbell and Mark Hosenball, an American journalist who worked for *Time Out*. As a result of this article, Mark Hosenball, along with a former CIA agent called Philip Agee, were deported.

4   'Minutes of Housmans Board Meeting 7 December 1974',
    Housmans Archive, Housmans Minute Book 1972–83.

Crispin Aubrey, who was also a journalist at *Time Out*, campaigned against the deportation of his colleague. In February 1977, Crispin and Duncan Campbell, who wrote the original article, met with John Berry, a social worker who had once been a corporal in signals intelligence. All three were arrested as they left the meeting and charged under the Official Secrets Act. Presumably the police knew about their meeting because they were intercepting Duncan Campbell's phone calls.

The trial of the trio became known as the 'ABC' trial — for Aubrey, Berry, Campbell. They faced harsh prison sentences of up to fourteen years if convicted of Section I of the Act, a draconian law usually reserved for people spying for foreign powers. The ABC trial generated a lot of publicity and was covered extensively in the mainstream press. It was big news, as Crispin Aubrey's wife Sue Aubrey pointed out, partly because 'it was about journalists, so other journalists are interested in that, because it was [about] freedom of the press.'

A defence campaign began to support the defendants. It met above pubs and used Campaign Against Arms Trade's office at 5 Cally Road to organise and work on the campaign. Sue Aubrey joined the defence campaign after the arrest of her husband and 'was catapulted into a world I didn't have any experience of really'. Political organising felt intimidating and unfamiliar, although Sue had been on protests and involved in grassroots community work before. She had been part of groups that had campaigned to stop their allotments being built on, organised a local playgroup, started a nursery and volunteered at an advice centre in Hackney, where they lived. At an early meeting to support the campaign she remembers people saying:

'Oh, this is a conspiracy theory' ... And I thought, I don't even know what this means ... And people were saying, 'It's political.' And I thought, what does that mean? You know, because it was all completely out of my world.

She explained why they needed an office space for the defence campaign:

Campaigning in 1977 was completely different from today, because there were no computers, there was no social media. So, if you wanted to get people out, we had to have things like telephone trees ... where you had somebody at the top of a list who perhaps had three people to contact, and then each of those three people contact three people, and so on. So, by the time you got to the bottom you could have a lot of people contacted. That's the sort of principle of it anyway.

To get the word out they would make leaflets:

Somebody would have to draft the words, somebody else would do the design. And then you would have to have a list of people who would deliver them. And we'd encourage people to go on our mailing lists, so things were sent out by post all the time. That doesn't happen now, because of social media ... And that's what we would have been doing in Housmans. You were opening letters that had come into *Time Out* about the campaign, and responding to them if you could, and updating the mailing list. My memory is that we had sheets and sheets of A4 paper divided into probably ten squares, and then you had people's names and addresses. And then you had to update it if people moved or whatever. And then we photocopied each page, and then cut out the addresses and then stuck them on envelopes.

**Sue and Crispin Aubrey had a three-year-old child, with another born during the defence campaign. Sue had limited time for office work, but she would bring the children to all the events:**

We went to the Post Office Tower, and we let hot air balloons up. And of course, children were very much involved in that, because they really enjoyed that. The reason it was the Post Office Tower was because it was all to do with signals intelligence. And also, that was connected with Cheltenham and GCHQ, which had never been publicised up until the ABC campaign. So, all that was quite new. And one Sunday we went out to Cheltenham [where GCHQ was based] and marched round there. So, anything which was marching or something, the children were obviously part of as well.

By now, Albert Beale had recovered from the BWNIC trial and was again working for *Peace News* as its London worker. He attended the ABC case committal hearing at Tottenham Magistrates Court in November 1977, when the prosecution had to show there was enough evidence to try the case in the crown court. At this hearing, they heard from an anonymous expert witness, 'Colonel B', whose evidence was meant to show that the information that Crispin Aubrey and Duncan Campbell discussed could have been a serious danger to the state if it had been made public. Albert said he was 'tipped off' about where to find out the Colonel's real identity in army records in the

Appeal for support for *Peace News* and *The Leveller*

PEACE NEWS NEEDS YOUR HELP

Both Peace News and the Leveller have now heard that they are to be prosecuted for contempt of Court following their publishing of the name of Colonel B in a recent court hearing. Colonel B is Colonel H.A. Johnstone. The costs of this case could be enourmous and possibly crippling. COME TO OUR MEETING and meet ONE OF THE EDITORS FROM PEACE NEWS. It's at Grapevine Cafe, 178 Oxford Road, Manchester which is near the University and the Polytechnic. Come on Wednesday March 12th at 8.00pm.

If you have any ideas about raising money or other offers of support please contact Steve Bowers, 168 Hamilton Road, Longsight Manchester 13 or ring 061-224-2566.

public domain, using the evidence he had given in court. Colonel B's real name, Colonel H A Johnstone, was revealed in *Peace News* and *The Leveller*, a monthly magazine.

Albert recalled:

And then all hell broke loose. There was a big kerfuffle. The police started running around saying you are all in contempt of court, you are all going to be done for this, that and the other.

Meanwhile the real identity of Colonel B was becoming 'a cause celebre'. 'Colonel H A Johnstone' was spraypainted on walls and he was even named in Parliament by some supportive MPs. Albert remembered watching the news in the Prince Albert, the pub close to 5 Cally Road, after a meeting of the ABC defence campaign:

We were watching the news and at the beginning of the bulletin one of the headlines was 'MPs today name the secret witness,' you know, shock horror. We were all going, very good, get another pint. It then turned out ... the then Attorney General issued a ruling claiming, rather spuriously, that although those words had been spoken in Parliament, because the witness was a secret, then reporting that part of Parliament would not be covered by Parliamentary privilege, which was bullshit but that's what the Attorney General did to try and stop the media reporting it. At the end of that half hour news bulletin I remember sitting waiting for the same headline to come round at the end ... and the newsreader at the end of the bulletin starts saying 'And today in Parliament, four MPs said that' and then another piece of paper was slapped down in front of him, on camera, on air, and he has a quick glance at it and he tries to integrate it into his script, 'Apparently the Attorney General has just announced that despite being named in Parliament, the media are not allowed to report that the secret witness was Col H A—oh whoops I'd better not say that'. This was all live on air, which brought the house down.

The Attorney General did not manage to stop the media reporting the identity of 'Colonel B'. However, charges of criminal contempt were brought against *Peace News* and *The Leveller*. Albert chose to defend himself in the High Court and gave the Lord Chief Justice 'a lecture on various Gandhian precepts which went down quite well in some of the media coverage of the case but didn't get me off'. All the individual defendants and the magazines, most of whom had had a barrister arguing their case, were found guilty of criminal contempt. In 1979 the Law Lords overturned this verdict after a successful appeal by *Peace News* and *The Leveller*.

The ABC trial concluded in October 1978, when the defendants were found guilty of a less serious charge under Section 2 of the Official Secrets Act. No one went to prison. After the trial, Sue and Crispin Aubrey and their family moved out of London with John Berry, the ex-army officer, and his family, while Duncan Campbell continued working as an investigative journalist. A few years after the trial, Campbell

ABC trial at the Old Bailey, 1978. Duncan Campbell, Crispin Aubrey and John Berry accused of breaching the Official Secrets Act, on the first day of their trial

published a book about the government's preparations for nuclear war, while Crispin Aubrey campaigned for many years against a third reactor at Hinckley Point nuclear power station.[5]

Albert thought that hosting the defence campaigns at 5 Cally Road 'kept the politics of the place on the go rather nicely'. It was certainly important for the people involved that they had a sympathetic place from which to organise. Sue reflected that 5 Cally Road:

Was an important place to be based, even if it was just for a short period of time. My memory of it seemed to encapsulate campaigning really and allowing people to have space in order to do that. Because there can't be many places, even now, which are like that.

5    'Crispin Aubrey Legacy', *The Crispin Aubrey Legacy Fund*
     <http://www.crispinaubrey.org/anti-nuclear-campaigner.
     html> [accessed 10 May 2022].

## Housmans is Attacked

Although it was felt to be a safe place by many of the people who used it, the building's status as a left-wing base also made it a target. A few months before the ABC trial was resolved, in the summer of 1978, the building came under attack again, this time from the far right. Jim Huggon remembered:

> We had a letter from a neo-Nazi group saying they were going to send us a bomb. It was printed, I remember, on beautiful Swastika letterhead. And we tried to handle it carefully, and gave it to the Bomb Squad, and they didn't do anything with it.

A meeting was called of tenants at 5 Cally Road that considered the risks of a right-wing attack. Minutes of a Housmans board meeting reported that 'steps had been taken to improve security by reinforcing the side entrance, closing the shop door letter box, adding a further fire extinguisher for inflammable liquids'.[6] Despite these extra precautions, on 4 July 1978 a letter bomb which had been addressed to 5 Caledonian Road exploded, injuring bookshop worker Stewart Porte. Stewart was hospitalised with burns for several weeks before recovering and returning to work in the shop.

Having a bomb explode inside the building, and injure one of the people that worked there, must have brought the general sense of threat to a new level for those involved in the building, especially when combined with news of the many other radical bookshops and left-wing organisations that were attacked by far-right groups at this time.

Police and crowd outside 5 Caledonian Road

6     'Minutes of Housmans Board Meeting 10 March 1978', Housmans Archive, Housmans Minute Book 1972–83.

# CHAPTER 5

# KEEPING THE LIGHTS ON

The 24 hour information and advice service for lesbians and gay men

## Switchboard

While the building was being bombed, raided and threatened with legal action in the 1970s, 'London Gay Switchboard' continued to operate.[1] Switchboard was a constant presence in the building from 1974 until they left for new, purpose-built premises in 1993.

From 1975 Switchboard volunteers kept the phone lines open 24 hours a day. Four phone lines were installed in the small room, with the handsets installed on one long table that ran along the wall. The volunteers, who were carefully selected and intensively trained, kept logbooks where they recorded every call so that the next shift of volunteers could take over where they had left off.

Switchboard was (and still is) often the first point of call for people who had never spoken about their sexuality before. It was life-changing for many of the people who called.

Mike Jackson was born in 1954 in Accrington, 'a small industrial working-class town' in Lancashire. He remembered his grandmother, 'a fierce Labour supporter' who despised working-class Tories as a strong political influence on him. He wanted to work in horticulture and by the age of 19 was studying at Kew, in London. He said:

> [I was] struggling with my sexuality. I mean, I knew since I came out of the womb, I think that I was gay. But I didn't come from a very intellectual or liberal tradition, and I was absolutely terrified about my own sexuality. I was hiding it. And I absorbed, I'm afraid, all the homophobic nonsense that there was around me, that I was a mad, sad and bad person.

Finding a small advert for London Gay Switchboard in *Time Out*, not long after the helpline opened, he decided to call:

> Such was my paranoia about being out, that I looked for a telephone box that was a long way from where any of the other Kew students could possibly walk, fearful that they might suddenly spring the door of the telephone kiosk open and go, 'Haha! you're a homosexual. Got ya!' Anyway, I found this telephone kiosk, and I'm sure it wouldn't have been one telephone call that kind of made me see different; I'm pretty sure I was saying to them, 'I know you don't think there's anything wrong with being an 'omosexual, but I do!' in that kind of strong Lancashire accent. And then I think one time I just realised that if you stop banging your head on the wall, it stops hurting, and I just suddenly thought, maybe they're right, maybe there is nothing wrong with it.

1    In 1986 it was renamed London Lesbian and Gay
Switchboard, but for ease it will be referred to here as
'Switchboard', the name it has at the time of writing.

And I think the pivotal thing was one of them eventually said, 'Look, there is nothing wrong with you; there *is* something wrong, it's called homophobia. So, homosexuality is not wrong and bad; homophobia is dreadful, and that's why you feel bad about yourself. It's that that we need to fight.' And once that penny dropped, I went from being this rather depressed, scared youngster, into being incandescently happy and angry at the same time. And I was enjoying an active guilt-free sex life, I was liberated. But I also got very, very political with it, because I suddenly got all this resentment and anger about all this nonsense that I had been fed since childhood. So, my sexuality really became the centre of my political activism. I didn't abandon socialism, why would I, but it wasn't as imperative. And so, I got involved in gay politics, I suppose you could call it.

Newspaper advert for London Gay Switchboard

Mike then went to Keele University, where he helped set up a Gay Switchboard on campus. He returned to London in 1980 and joined London Gay Switchboard as a volunteer in 1983. As a prospective volunteer he was interviewed by two existing members of Switchboard, who assessed his knowledge of the gay scene in detail. One of his interviewers was Mark Ashton. Mike and Mark would become friends and a year later, in 1984, they co-founded the group Lesbians and Gays Support the Miners after collecting money for the miners at that year's Pride march.

During the day all the phone lines were staffed, at night just one.[2] The volunteer staying overnight would sleep on a mattress with the phone close to their head, ready to wake and take a call if need be. Volunteers committed to a certain number of shifts a month, including overnight stays. Mike explained:

> It was the only switchboard in the world that offered that 24/7 service. So, we had lots of international callers. I've taken calls from Beirut, Australia, the States, Latin America, et cetera. But it was always tough doing the overnight thing, because obviously the volume of phone calls would dwindle to hardly any, so between say, two in the morning and seven in the morning you might get two or three calls. And I actually fell asleep on a caller once, because I just wasn't used to being up all night. I don't think the caller realised.

It was 'wonderful', Mike said, to be able to return the support he'd been given years before:

> And the stories that you learnt about people's lives. I can say this now because it's many, many years ago. I had a call from a lesbian, who had just lost her partner, her partner had died, but the real story was that the two of them had had a closeted relationship for

---

2  In 1984 Switchboard installed a fifth phone line because of the amount of calls they received. However, due to lack of space it was only operated at peak times (*Capital Gay*, 24 August 1984).

Map in London Gay Switchboard office

decades. They had both got husbands, and they had both got children, and they would do all the necessary duties to maintain their families. And then, five days a week they would meet for a few hours midday. And that had gone on for years and years and years, they had kept that relationship completely secret. And I'm on the end of the phone just thinking, oh my God, this poor woman. I said, 'Am I the only person who knows that your partner's died?' And she said, 'Oh yes, and you always will be.' So, this woman had had to live with this grief, this bereavement, and not be able to share it with a single other human being. And I just thought, what amazing strength … But my God, that's only one of hundreds of thousands of stories that Switchboard volunteers could tell you.

Switchboard was run entirely by volunteers. Mike explained that as well as answering the phones, each volunteer had to take on another task to help maintain the organisation. All the information that Switchboard needed to share with its callers was written up, stored in the office and kept up to date by the volunteers. Mike chose to maintain the big map of the UK on the wall of the office where different kind of services and facilities for the gay community — everything from LGBTQ+ bars to sexual health clinics — were identified with a different coloured pin. Mark Ashton, on the other hand, volunteered to keep the religious file, despite being, as Mike said, a 'raving Marxist Communist':

And that says a lot about Mark. He would never, never dream of doing a disservice to the callers; people were phoning up, genuinely distressed trying to reconcile their sexuality with their religious beliefs, Roman Catholics particularly suffered in that area. And Mark would always make sure the information was up to date, and he would give good and helpful, and loving, counsel to anybody who was coming from that position. But, secretly, within the closed doors of the organisation, this red vinyl resource book, religious file, that he looked after, was absolutely plastered on the outside with communist iconography.

Taking calls

Julian Hows, who volunteered at Switchboard for nearly 20 years, described how Switchboard was the 'first point of call' for the LGBTQ+ community, not only for information as simple as finding a place to go out for the night, but also in emergency situations:

> When people got arrested [we were] their first line of emergency support to solicitors. And when [there was] a purge upon a particular pub, [the police] lining the customers up against the wall outside the Vauxhall Tavern, because they wanted to search everybody for drugs, and effectively it was a bit of homophobia too ... And the police coming in in their blue gloves, because of course we all had AIDS, you know? And somebody immediately phoning Switchboard and saying, 'Oh, the police have arrived, and they can't even wear matching shoes and gloves, darling.'

Not all calls were genuine, as another volunteer, Steve Craftman, described:

> On a busy shift, one individual could take 100 calls. Okay, thirty, forty of them [were] perhaps hoaxes. It really was the done thing in every office around the country, to leave a note on somebody's desk asking them to call Mr Hugh Janus.

In the early 1980s, as the AIDS epidemic began and increasing numbers of people began to get sick, Switchboard was often the place they turned to for advice. Diana James, who volunteered at Switchboard in the 1980s and early 1990s said the most difficult calls often came at night:

> Sometimes you'd get the suicide calls, and you'd get people phoning in that were really suffering badly with AIDS and were in a lot of pain, a lot of discomfort. Or their partner had just recently died, and they were frightened of losing their home. They weren't allowed to go to the funeral. They weren't mentioned in the will.

Steve Craftman explained that even if callers had contacted them about something else, during the AIDS epidemic:

> They got the condom lecture. We were very proactive in advice about safer sex ... Information was spotty, difficult to come by, and for the majority of people, Switchboard was the canonical source. A new magazine would come in from the US, and we'd be picking it apart for every last scrap of information.
>
> I think it was dated [1985], an entry I made in the logbooks, after I had had a call from a guy who had been diagnosed with KS [Kaposi's Sarcoma], which was an AIDS diagnosis. That morning [he] was intending committing suicide. He was a healthcare worker, knew the attitudes of healthcare workers towards people with AIDS. And he was getting progressively drunker and drunker. I ended up having an explosion in the logbooks. You know, nothing in any of the training that I've had in this organisation prepared me for this. We need to do more.

At work in the London Gay Switchboard office

In response to Steve's logbook entry, Switchboard set up support groups to talk about how the AIDS pandemic was affecting them, something that became increasingly vital as volunteers themselves tested positive and experienced the loss of friends and colleagues. In 1987, Steve tested positive for HIV. He thinks he was the first person to come out within Switchboard as HIV positive. Meanwhile, Switchboard, along with the rest of the LGBTQ+ community, lost many people to the disease. Among them was Mark Ashton, who died on 11 February 1987 at the age of 27.

All of this important and often difficult work took place in conditions that were not always ideal, as Steve Craftman described:

> You take probably the busiest lesbian and gay organisation in the country, push it into a space the size of a small flat. That's what it was like. It was run down; we were running

London Gay Switchboard workers on the stairs in 5 Caledonian Road it down faster ... One of the things that became more important, well should have been important from the start, but was emphasised by HIV, was those stairs were bloody murder. You know, we had a chain ladder kept in the phone room; that was the fire escape.

Switchboard did not advertise their address as there was a very real risk of attack from far-right groups like the National Front. Ann Feltham, who worked at Campaign Against Arms Trade in the 1980s, remembers 'it was drummed into us that we didn't tell anybody Switchboard was in the building.'

Steve Craftman explained:

Switchboard had a buzzer to get in. Just no way could everybody have a key. Security was a big issue because of anti-gay feeling at the time; the address was kept secret. I used to get annoyed at people who, hearing the buzzer go in the phone room, would just automatically buzz somebody in.

Diana James said:

I think it's difficult for people now to realise the threat that lesbian and gay organisations were under at that time. Because when we were leaving after a shift at Housmans, we would come down to the front door, which was at the side [of the building], and we would have a little hole in the paper that covered it. And we would look through that to see if there was anyone waiting for us outside. Because we had had volunteers beaten up before, and some quite badly. So, of a necessity we had to be really careful leaving and entering the building.

Switchboard's constant presence in the building could make it safer for the other people who used it; there was always someone in. Julian Hows remembered a time he sought refuge at Switchboard before he volunteered there himself. In 1974 Julian started work as a Tube guard on the London Underground.[3] In 1976 women were allowed to become guards for the first time, thanks to the Sex Discrimination Act that had passed into law the previous year. As women could choose to wear either trousers or skirts as their uniform, Julian made a formal request to be able to choose to wear the female guards' uniform if he wished. He says it 'started as a bit of a joke' but continued to press for it for two years, with the support of his union. He had an official meeting at London Transport Headquarters, where they offered him time off if he wanted to transition to be a woman, which Julian says was 'very radical for an employer at the time'. However, they refused his request to be able to wear a skirt as a man.

3    'Julian Hows: A Tube Guard's Pioneering LGBT+ Gender Protest', *London Transport Museum* <https://www.ltmuseum.co.uk/collections/stories/people/julian-hows-tube-guards-pioneering-lgbt-gender-protest> [accessed 21 May 2022].

In 1978 Julian decided to resign 'but make a big splash about it', so he invited the press to come and see him wearing a female guard's uniform on his last day at work at Earl's Court Station. He ended up on the television news, who were supposed to send a car to take him safely home to Brixton, but no car turned up.

Julian explained:

So, I phoned up Switchboard, and actually got through. I explained my situation, I said, 'Look, I know where you are, and I know where the building is, and I've been there before. And I know you're not supposed to meet callers. But can I just sit there, in the corner for an hour or so, until friends that I know are going to end up at the GLF disco [at the Prince Albert] ... at the top of the road. So, very sweetly, they broke all the rules, and said, 'Yes, sure, come along.' So, I sat for an hour listening to the calls, until the disco had opened and I could go up the road, and, people had brought me up a change of clothes and I could have a beer.

When Campaign Against Arms Trade (CAAT) moved out of the building to new offices in 1986, Switchboard rented the room they had vacated on the first floor. This was the George Lansbury room, originally named after the pacifist Labour politician and campaigner. Steve Craftman renamed Switchboard's new room 'Angela Lansbury', after George Lansbury's granddaughter:

I was the one [who] renamed it Angie's, Angela's room. I was a big fan of Sondheim, and she was the first Mrs Lovett in Sweeney Todd. I have never knowingly seen an episode of Murder She Wrote. I hadn't heard of George Lansbury before, and it was only curiosity on my part that led me to find out the link between the two.

In fact, they were not the first to rename the George Lansbury room. Lesley Mair, who had worked at CAAT earlier in the decade, had decided 'all the rooms shouldn't be named after blokes', and had christened it the 'Catherine Marshall Room' after 'a heroine of the First World War peace movement'.

Julian thought that Switchboard renaming the room 'Angela Lansbury' was noticed:

> I think some of the more laid-back members of the [building's] management, thought [that] was a little bit cheeky. However, that's queers, you know, they're all right really, but they do push the buttons sometimes.

While Switchboard volunteers got on well with the other people who used the building, there were clearly some differences. Lesley Mair remembered overhearing a Switchboard volunteer showing a new recruit around the building, joking 'And in this office it's the Campaign Against Arms Trade, another well-meaning lost cause.'

Julian reflected that being based at 5 Cally Road might have helped keep Switchboard focused on its 'core function' of running the helpline. The 'constraints of the building' (its lack of space) meant that other projects 'spawned' by Switchboard had to 'float off' elsewhere:

> We were never going to meet callers, you know? We were never going to do x or y or z. We were not going to have a newspaper. We were not going to take over, as one person suggested, the London Lesbian and Gay Centre. And to a certain extent ... that whole thing of having a peppercorn rent, a small squeeze space, allowed us to develop ... And the physicality of the space actually put volunteers together. They had to talk to each other, you know?

There were also serious drawbacks to working in such a small space. In 1984, on their tenth anniversary, Switchboard launched a 'Put Your Money Where Our Mouth Is' campaign to raise £100,000 within two years to buy their own offices.[4] At the time there were fears that 5 Cally Road would be demolished due to developments planned for the area (see Chapters 7 and 8.) *Gay Times* reported that the offices at 5 Cally Road were too 'cramped' to expand Switchboard's services, 'there are only four small rooms to work from, and when meetings are held these usually overflow onto the stairs.'[5]

4 '£100,000!', *Gay News*, 26 August 1984, p. 100.
5 'Gay Switchboard to Raise £100,000', *Gay Times*, September 1984.

In October 1988 Switchboard became the proud owners of a building near King's Cross, although they needed to raise another £300,000 to convert it to their needs. They would finally move into their new, specially adapted home in 1993.

Diana James argued that without 5 Cally Road giving them a low rent home for almost two decades:

> Switchboard might have existed but certainly not as it is, without 5 Cally Road. Without them giving that space, then I rather doubt that Switchboard would exist as it does. Might not have actually got off the ground, possibly. So, that's huge. Switchboard has been going forty-five years, it's still there, it's still working, it's still doing the stuff, it's still saving young people's lives. Someone in Arbroath or someone in the wilds of the countryside phones up Switchboard because it's the first place they can come out; it's the first place they can talk about maybe the abuse they are facing; it's the first place they can go to find out where they can go to meet other people like themselves. Switchboard is vital in those respects. Switchboard has saved lives, so, if 5 Cally Road hadn't been there to help set Switchboard up, or give it a place, how many lives would we have lost?

Leaflet advertising the return of the GLF disco to the Prince Albert pub

# CHAPTER    6

# ANARCHY, PEACE
# AND FREEDOM

The early 1980s were busy years for peace campaigners. Cruise missiles were arriving in the country. Britain went to war over the Falkland Islands. Many of the groups based in or connected to 5 Cally Road campaigned around both issues.

There was change inside the building too, Harry Mister retired as General Manager of the bookshop and building in 1981, after which Housmans was run by a collective of bookshop workers. As just one of many radical bookshops around the country, and no longer so deeply connected to *Peace News*, now the paper was well established in Nottingham, Housmans began to forge a new identity for itself.

## Peace

In 1979 the threat of nuclear war loomed closer when both NATO and the Soviet Union established new missile bases in Europe. In the UK the new Conservative government, headed by Margaret Thatcher, agreed to place cruise missiles at two military bases, Greenham and Molesworth, for the United States. Separately, the British government decided to renew the UK's nuclear weaponry, replacing the now ageing Polaris system with Trident.

In response, a new wave of protest against nuclear weapons grew and CND along with it. The movement held large demonstrations and nonviolent direct actions. There were dozens of protest camps set up around the country, the most famous and long lasting being the women's camp at Greenham Common.

The resurgence of the nuclear disarmament movement was promising for 5 Cally Road. In 1981 a Housmans board meeting hoped that the 'the present upsurge of movement activity provided an appropriate time [for the bookshop] to try out new ideas'. One new idea by some of the bookshop workers was to make links with young punks who were becoming politicised through the anarcho-punk scene. There were other new opportunities to promote the bookshop. One was Glastonbury festival, which in 1981 was struggling and joined forces with CND, who helped to promote it to their mailing list of 350,000 people.[1] Housmans happily provided a book stall at this and subsequent festivals.

*Peace News* used its London worker (then Albert Beale) to report on the peace camps, providing a valuable service of 'rounding-up' news from all the camps every fortnight, as he described:

> I would be ringing round contacts all over the country and doing a page round up every fortnight of who was doing what. It was a little bit tedious in a sense but there was a way in which in that era, *Peace News* was almost a paper of record [of what was happening in the camps].

Women dance around their 15 foot maypole atop the weapons silo on Mayday at RAF Cottesmore, Rutland

However, at the same time as the nuclear disarmament movement was growing, *Peace News'* circulation remained low (it was 4,500 in 1984,) while Housmans began losing money for the first time. A working group was set up in 1984 to consider why this was the case. They reported that *Peace News* and Housmans seemed to be 'stuck in a rut; that we seem to be not responding to nor receiving energy from that resurgence of peace movement activity'.[2]

In April 1982 Britain went to war with Argentina over the Falkland Islands. The undeclared war lasted ten weeks; 900 people died. *Peace News* gave extensive critical coverage of the war, while groups connected to 5 Cally Road like Pax Christi, London

1    'CND at Glastonbury: The Beginning ', 2020 <https://cnduk.org/cnd-at-glastonbury-at-the-beginning/> [accessed 2 June 2022].

2    'Report of the Peace News Trustees Working Group, April 1984', 1984, University of Bradford Special Collections, Archives of *Peace News* Cwl/PN/5/11.

## GENOCIDE IN LEBANON p7

# peace news
## for nonviolent revolution

No 2173  Friday 25 June 1982
FORTNIGHTLY

**30p**

THATCHER'S

HERO

NAVY CUT

HARD ROCK ∗ STOPPING SIZEWELL ∗ CO-OPS CO-OPTED?
ANIMAL RIGHTS ∗ N-WASTE DUMPING IN WALES ∗ REVIEWS IN BRIEF

5, CALEDONIAN ROAD, KINGS CROSS, LONDON N1 9DX
(01 - 278 1976)

NEWSLETTER 54

19 May 1982

# Raise facts, not flags

Because Britain has sold a substantial amount of military, and almost exclusively naval, equipment to Argentina, CAAT has been very much in demand by the media, organisations, groups and individuals. Within five days of the invasion of the Falkland Islands CAAT had produced a factsheet on the British military involvement in Argentina, giving full details of sales and background information on training and the missiles and helicopters. A few days later, the National Peace Council produced a most comprehensive historical background with proposals for a solution. Details of availability of both are on page 3.

CAAT's press release accompanying the factsheet led to, amongst others, an interview on Radio 4's "Today" programme to which the Defence Sales Organisation were invited but, significantly, refused to attend.

Never before, it seems, has Britain been involved in a war for which the arms salesmen and advertisers have been more to blame than the politicians and generals. Arms salesmen like wars for two reasons:- the equipment gets test marketed and improvements can be made, and they do nicely out of the ensuing re-armament. They have been preparing for war for years. It is Lord Carrington and his ilk who have been taken by surprise. (For more on the arms sellers see page 2.) So it is no wonder, then that the DSO wants to keep such a low profile

Since the start of the crisis there has been a deafening silence in the British media on at least two issues which need a much higher profile:-

1. The Defence Sales Organisation has excelled in its efforts to arm the world, and make sure that every time someone is blown up, drowned, burned or maimed, its done with quality British equipment and none of your foreign rubbish - and that "our" manufacturers make as much cash out of it as possible. Yet nowhere has there been serious discussion about its clear culpability.

● The Falklands crisis isn't far away but here in electronics companies in the home counties and in offices like the DSO. Make sure that you point this out when writing to your local press, seeing your MP or whatever else you are doing to resist the Falklands madness.

2. The British Army Equipment Exhibition 82 (BAEE) has likewise largely been overlooked in the glories of the retaking of South Georgia and the ignominies of the sinking of the cruiser *Belgrano*. It has been planned for 21-25 June in Aldershot and as far as we know at this time, there is no intention of cancelling it. But in the present situation this could very well be possible and there are lots of ideas and suggestions for things you can do on page 3.

Several MPs responded quickly to a special CAAT mailing to them on the Falklands and BAEE and asked about cancellation. From the length and tone of the replies we have seen, it seems as though the government is indeed worried about how it will 'look', and realise at last that we do have a point about the inappropriateness of BAEE going ahead in the middle of a UN Special Session on Disarmament AND a war!

● If you do nothing else, please write to the Prime Minister and send a copy to Michael Foot, calling for BAEE to be cancelled. It needs your continued pressure now.

Further analysis of the arms aspects of the crisis appears on page 2, but here is another angle you could work on.

Both parties to the Falklands conflict are armed not only with British but also French weapons. If Venezuela and Chile and Brazil are drawn more directly into the conflict (on whatever side) even more weapons will be used against others from the same manufacturer. CAAT will provide you with the details, but please send a s.a.e. Contacts in other major arms supplier countries have been approached to sign a statement we have written condemning all conventional arms sales.

Write to your Member of ●
the European Parliament to ask them to urge that the trade in arms does not carry on as if nothing had happened.

*(montage by CAAT)*

Greenpeace and Campaign Against Arms Trade (CAAT) campaigned against it. Lesley Mair, who worked for CAAT in 5 Cally Road at the time, remembered what she did when war broke out:

In 1982, we found ourselves in the position where this country, within the space of about four days, turned from being completely unaware of where the Falkland Islands were, to ... a very jingoistic mood ...

I was actually on my own, and I remember, it was a Sunday night, and I was just thinking, Do you know what, I'm going to get a lot of questions about British arms exports

**CAMPAIGN AGAINST ARMS TRADE**

5, CALEDONIAN ROAD, KINGS CROSS, LONDON N1 9DX
(01 - 278 1976)

CAAT FACTSHEET 32

BRITISH MILITARY INVOLVEMENT IN ARGENTINA

(UPDATED VERSION)

5p

MILITARY EQUIPMENT SUPPLIED TO OR ORDERED BY ARGENTINA

Major weapons ( aircraft, armoured vehicles and heavy artillery, missiles and warships)

1 second hand aircraft carrier, *"Colossus"*. Supply date uncertain.
6 second hand coastal minesweepers. Supply date uncertain.
2 Type 42 frigates, *Hercules* and *Santissima Trinidad*. One built in Argentina under licence from Vickers.
Seacat ship-to-air missiles made by Short Brothers Ltd of Belfast. Supply date uncertain.
12 Sea Dart ship-to-air missiles made by British Aerospace. Supply date uncertain.
          Probably made in Hatfield and/or Bolton.
20 Tigercat surface-to-air missiles, 10 to Marines, 10 to Army, made by Short Brothers Ltd of Belfast.
10 Lynx helicopters from Westland Aircraft Ltd of Yeovil. Ordered 1977 and 1979. Total 6 delivered.
Shorland armoured cars for the gendarmerie. Made by Short Brothers Ltd of Belfast. Supply date and no. uncertain.
9 Canberra B62 bomber aircraft. Ordered early 1970s. Number delivered uncertain.

Military equipment not classified as major weapons

100 sub machine guns from Sterling Armament Co., Dagenham, Essex. (Five with 'silencers'). 1975
Ferranti 'Isis' sights for Argentine Air Force Skyhawk(US) aircraft. Made in Bracknell. 1976.
Ferranti 'Seaspray' radar for Lynx helicopters. Made in Edinburgh. 1977
Decca 'Clearscan' radar for fast patrol boats. Made in Walton on Thames. 1979
Redifon HF and VHF radio systems for coastal partol boats. Made in London SW18. 1979
Vickers gear pumps for West German built frigates. Made in Barrow. Ordered 1980
Rediffusion Radio Systems further radio transmitters for naval stations. Made in Surbiton. Ordered 1981
Rolls-Royce engines for Italian built jet trainer aircraft. Some reported sighted but delivery uncertain. 1981
Doncasters Moorside 'Morgrip' bolts for propellors on naval vessels. Made in Oldham. Ordered Sept/Oct 1981
Racal-Decca electronic support measures (ESM) for eavesdropping on radio and radar. Ordered Sept/Oct 1981
Smiths Industries 250 Mach/airspeed indicators for Argentinian-built counter insurgency aircraft.
          Ordered Sept/Oct 1981
Vosper Thornycroft pneumatic controls for patrol boats and corvettes. Ordered Sept/Oct 1981
Blowpipe man-portable supersonic anti-aircraft missiles made by Short Brothers Ltd of Belfast. Ordered 1981
Plessey Ferranti modifications for Type 42 frigates. Done in the late 1970s in the UK.

The military equipment supplied by Britain has been almost exclusively naval, apart from the Shorland armoured cars and the Tigercat and Blowpipe missiles. The value of the sales for the last five years has been:-
 (£ million) 1977 £0.7; 1978 £4.9; 1979 £62.6; 1980 £46.7; 1981 £12.5
Other countries supplying arms to Argentina over the period 1977-81 were:- West Germany 33%, USA 17%, France 15%, Israel 14%. Britain was the next largest supplying 10%
Following the arms ban imposed by President Carter, Argentina has looked to European countries to supply the licences and designs to enable it to move towards self sufficiency in arms. Argentina is now one of the major Third World arms producers. As far as information is available, a substantial number of the export lic-ences appear to have been issued under a Labour Government.
Argentinian forces personnel have been receiving military training in Britain since at least 1979. In 1981 some British forces personnel were also reported to be on loan or secondment to Argentina.
Argentina has attended Britain's annual military equipment show since at least 1978, sending delegations of between 7 and 12.

SOME POINTS ABOUT THE HELICOPTERS AND MISSILES

Lynx Called by its manufacturers, Westland Aircraft Ltd,"the most advanced helicopter of its class in the world".
   *"In two years time (ie 1982) it will be the finest fighting helicopter any country could want"* said the commanding officer of the Lynx's parent 702 squadron.*Flight International*, 9 August 1980.
   May be used for anti-submarine warfare and is in service on Type 42 frigates.
   Uses Ferranti Seaspray radar. Decca Tans computers and Decca electronic support measures.

Seacat A close range ship-to-air guided missile for anti-aircraft defence.
   Its makers, Short Brothers Ltd, describe it as "Britain's export best-seller in guided weapons".
   Flies with almost any radar system and can avoid radar detection by flying at zero altitude.

Tigercat Ground-to-air version of Seacat. Supplied to Argentinian Army and Marines.

Sea Dart Long range ship-to-air missile complementary to Seawolf. Manufacturers, British Aerospace, boast of its "high lethality" and "rapid reaction".
   Propelled by Rolls-Royce ram jet and used on Type 42 frigates and fast patrol boats.
   Made by British Aerospace Dynamics.

to Argentina. What I'll do is, I'll make my life easier, I'll produce a factsheet, and then if anybody asks me, I'll just give them the factsheet. And then I thought, yeah, I'll do a press release as well. So, I did a press release to accompany that factsheet, and it was taken up by Radio 4, the *Today* programme, and they said, 'Oh could you come and talk about this?' So, I went down to be interviewed ... about British arms exports. I think that was probably the first time CAAT had got national publicity at that level.

That was a very busy time, speaking in Hyde Park, and whatever. And [in 5 Cally Road] ... a small group of people got together to organise anti-Falklands War protests. ...

And I remember going down to the police station ... just off Downing Street, with Mark James from Pax Christi, and talking to the police about the routes we were going to follow, and how we were going to steward it, and so on. And then, there was that march from Hyde Park down to ... Trafalgar Square. So Caledonian Road was really quite involved in the anti-Falklands War activities.

5 Cally Road was, Lesley reflected, a safe space to organise an unpopular campaign like this. Campaigners felt:

isolated ... we got spat at on this protest march ... And we knew that we were a minority, but ... we were with like-minded people, and there was no question of having to argue the position with people who worked at Housmans Bookshop. I mean, it was all taken for granted. So in a way, at the time, we needed each other, and it was quite supportive. And I think maybe if the Campaign Against Arms Trade had been functioning from just an office block somewhere else, it might have felt very threatening; but [5 Cally Road] was a very safe place to be, because you knew that anybody coming in the door was going to be thinking the same as you.

## Anarcho-punk

Malcolm Hopkins started working at Housmans in 1980. Already an experienced bookseller, he saw an opportunity for Housmans in the anarcho-punk scene that was connecting a new, younger generation with radical politics. One of these younger people was Ramsey Kanaan, a teenager in Scotland who got into punk early. By the age of thirteen he knew he was an anarchist:

> I remember going into the local record shop … And they had a t-shirt by this band called Crass, who were this (now legendary) anarcho-punk band who basically spawned the whole anarcho-punk movement or call it what you will. And I'd never heard the band Crass, I'd never heard their music, but the t-shirt had on it 'Anarchy, Peace and Freedom', like those three words as a slogan slashed across the t-shirt. And I thought, that's what I'm into.

Ramsey reflected that:

> the staple of punk was being kind of anti, they were against authority, they didn't like the police, they didn't like their parents, they didn't like getting old, they didn't like previous generations.

The same year Ramsey discovered Crass, he went on his first CND march.

Crass put on a benefit gig for *Peace News* in Exeter in 1982 and Housmans provided a bookstall for the gig. Sandy Donaldson remembered going on the road to help with bookstalls at Crass gigs, which could be 'rather rough and edgy'. The bookstall was splattered with blood at one gig in Digbeth Town Hall but in Exeter the stall was 'mobbed' between the music. Afterwards the bookshop workers reported back to the board that 'they felt the bookshop should do more to attract the radicals on the pop scene'.[3]

In December 1982, Ramsey went to see Crass and other anarcho-punk bands like Poison Girls, Flux of Pink Indian and Conflict at the Zig Zag Club:

> Crass and their cohorts squatted this still functioning club, I guess it still had electricity, apparently it still had beer on tap. So, they brought in a sound system and set up this massive all-day concert … Like many of these historic landmark events there weren't actually many people there, but you know, it's one of the things that if you interviewed 5,000 people, they'd all say they were there, but there was actually probably no more than a couple of hundred people … there. I can say that because I was one of them …
>
> And I was already involved in disseminating ideas, shall we say, in my … youthful fashion … I had my plastic bag full of fanzines and I was wandering around kind of annoying the concert-goers. 'Hey Mister, d'you want to buy a fanzine?' … and then I espied in the corner of the venue, a bunch of what to me were these really weird old dudes with

beards, which put me off because I was a young punk rocker and old people with beards are not ... what you'd normally gravitate towards, shall we say. And of course, in retrospect they were probably only ten years older than I was or maybe fifteen years older. But anyway, nevertheless they were sitting behind a table of literature and while I may have been put off by their hirsuteness, I nevertheless thought that this is the way to go ... I thought these guys have the right idea. Not only are they getting to sit down and have a much bigger spread than I could have out of a plastic bag, but people can come to them, you know what I mean? They don't have to go up and like harass everyone. So being the precocious little kid that I was, I went up to them and said, who are you, what are you doing, what's this, and asked them a million questions. And it transpires they were from Housmans, and they were doing a literature table at this squatted venue, this one-off gig.

After the Zig Zag club gig, Ramsey visited the bookshop every school holiday. He was already starting his own anarchist publishing and distribution venture, AK Press. Staff at Housmans, especially Malcolm Hopkins, helped him by teaching him about publishing and distribution:

largely by very patiently over the years answering my 5,000 questions and then patiently explaining it to me and in many cases materially helping me. So Housmans were the first people that gave me stuff in effect on consignment that wasn't from the fanzine punk world. They very generously [to] this unknown kid, basically said, okay, here's a bunch of stuff, you can take it from us, because we're the 'distributor', and we'll give you an invoice and you pay us whenever you sell it. So, you know, they were not only showing me how it's done but enabling me to do it.

As AK Press grew, Ramsey 'moved into Housmans basement', bringing as many boxes of books as he could manage down on the train to Kings Cross, then pushing them over to Housmans on a trolley. He said, 'so I think I went from being their kind of house mascot, being the little kid, to just being part of the furniture.'

Ramsey later brought out his first publication with the help of Malcolm Hopkins, a new edition of *The Catechism of a Revolutionist*, a manifesto for revolutionary secret societies written by Sergei Nechayev in 1869.

Ramsey described how 'because of my youth and enthusiasm' he was also willing to try and sell the 'dead stock' kept in the Housmans basement:

I'd take these old Tolstoy pamphlets that they'd published twenty years ago, and I was able to go and sell them. So, I was almost like this new generation of enthusiasm that was actually still disseminating, it's like the beauty of capitalism, right? If you can create

3    'Minutes of Housmans Board and Staff Meeting 22 September
     1982', Housmans Archive, Housmans Minute Book 1972–83.

a market for it, then you can sell it. If you can't, it's irrelevant. So that's the challenge of disseminating ideas, you have to get the ideas in front of people.

### The Housmans' Collective

At the beginning of the 1980s Housmans was in a period of adjustment and change. Harry Mister had retired, after more than forty-five years of work for the *Peace News* empire. He remained an active part of both the Housmans board and Peace News Trustees. After his retirement, Housmans was run by a collective of the staff, who were in turn overseen by the board.

Before leaving, Harry reviewed the progress the shop had made since 1959. The bookshop, he wrote, now took up six times more space then when they first opened. They had a new branch at Kingsway Princeton College nearby. There were six full-time and two part-time workers, although the low wages they were paid meant it was hard to keep staff for very long. Several staff members had left to work for other radical or alternative bookshops like Compendium books, the alternative bookshop in Camden Town. Housmans had always generally turned a profit, but it seemed that might be changing. Sales had been static between 1976 and 1979, while prices had risen. In the early 1980s the situation became worse when Housmans began suddenly to lose significant amounts of money for the first time, with a loss of £8,000 in the 1981—82 financial year.[4]

Rosie Ilett and 'Max' McLellan working in Housmans, 1983

In 1982 Rosie Ilett started work at Housmans. Just 22 years old when she joined, she was the only female member of staff. She was involved in the women's movement and had previously volunteered at Days of Hope, a radical bookshop in Newcastle. She said:

> I don't think I had ever heard of [Housmans] before then, but it seemed to be linked into lots of things I was interested in, like feminism, [the] peace movement. I suppose non-aligned sort of politics, like anarchist type politics. And, yes, the pay was pretty low, but that wasn't really an issue because my expenses for living were relatively low.

The shop seemed old fashioned to Rosie, 'like something out of the fifties in terms of the kind of layout'. It was 'a kind of ramshackle environment' and smelt musty — 'like going into somewhere where there were lots of boxes that hadn't been unpacked for years.' Cigarette smoke swirled in the air and there was always ash between the buttons on the till.

Rosie would work at times with Max (aka David) McLellan, who was in charge of the stationery section that still took up about a quarter of the shop, or help Malcolm Hopkins run the branch at the nearby Kingsway Princeton College down the road, where they sold academic books to help finance the rest of the shop. On the days Malcolm and Rosie went to the college, she remembers lugging heavy bags of academic textbooks down the road. In Housmans itself they sold:

> left-wing, feminist, socialist, peace movement, pacifist stuff ... books, pamphlets, political

postcards, posters, because of course that was how people got stuff like that. What else? Badges, millions of badges, that was a really big thing.

There were now over a hundred radical bookshops dotted across the country. In 1978, the bookshop told the board they had offered help to some of the newer shops, for instance giving some stock to a new Community Bookshop in Derry, a work experience placement to someone who wanted to run a bookshop in Bristol and financial advice to Sisterwrite, a feminist bookshop that opened close by.[5] The Housmans Board noted there were six other radical bookshops in the London Borough of Islington alone in 1979.[6] By 1981 this had risen to eight.[7] Housmans joined the Federation of Radical Booksellers in 1982, despite some reluctance from the board, who wanted the subscription fee to be justified (the bookshop workers signed them up anyway).[8]

In 1982, as Rosie was joining the staff, Housmans Distribution Service was set up to distribute books to other radical bookshops on a wholesale basis. They imported books to supply to other bookshops: radical books from Black Rose Press in Canada as well as the Gandhian literature they had always imported from India.[9] They specialised in books on nonviolent direct action, which they would also send to people by mail order.

The basement was used to pack books for distribution, as Rosie remembered:
I still love packing things to this very day. And every year we did the famous *Peace Diary*, which I think is still going. So that was a huge thing. So, in a day I might be on the till, or I might be doing packing downstairs, or I could be at the college, or sometimes we might do a bookstall somewhere.

5    'Minutes of Housmans Board Meeting 3 November 1978', Housmans Archive, Housmans Minute Book 1972–83.

6    'Minutes of Housmans Board and Staff Meeting 10 February 1979', Housmans Archive, Housmans Minute Book 1972–83.

7    'Minutes of Housmans Board and Staff Meeting 15 August 1981', Housmans Archive, Housmans Minute Book 1972–83.

8    'Minutes of Housmans Board and Staff Meeting 16 April 1982', Housmans Archive, Housmans Minute Book 1972–83.

9    In 1982 it emerged that Navajivan Press had sold Penguin the rights for a British edition of Gandhi's autobiography, which was being published in conjunction with a film about his life. Housmans had always been the sole distributor in the UK for Navajivan Press. Harry Mister encouraged the bookshop to see it as an opportunity to promote their Gandhian books [Minutes of Annual Meeting of Housmans Board, 29 October 1982, Housmans Archive.]

Nigel Kemp joined the bookshop staff in 1982 as the new bookkeeper, taking over from Jim Huggon. Nigel had been educated in private schools, studied at Oxford University, and had worked as an accountant for three years. In 1970 he went to an early GLF meeting at the LSE, which he says, 'transformed my life'. He remembered 5 Cally Road from his days in GLF, and when the vacancy at Housmans came up, his partner, Sandy Donaldson, encouraged him to apply.

Sandy grew up in a small industrial town in central Scotland. Homosexuality was still illegal in Scotland when he went to university, so after a year of studying he moved to London, where he met Nigel, who was then living in a GLF commune on a squatted street in Notting Hill. Sandy began working in typographic design and used these skills to help out Housmans by repainting the Housmans shop sign, laying out some of the pamphlets Housmans published and revamping the *Peace Diary*, as he explained:

There was the idea of the *Housmans Peace Diary* perhaps becoming something a bit more contemporary. Prior to that it had been a Collins commercial diary publication, which just had a bit stuck in the back, a signature or two in the back relating to that which contained the Housmans Peace Directory. And Collins produced this sort of thing for all sorts of people, like the Scouts Association. But in the ordinary commercial part of the diary, [there were] things that jarred rather with the Housmans peace thing, like the start of the grouse season, or all those sorts of odd bizarre dates they thought it would be good to have in this diary. And then, obviously there's a limit to what you could do with it. And there were other political diaries ... appearing, like the *Big Red Diary*, obviously competing with this one and making [it] rather outdated. So, there was the idea of producing something a bit more like that, where we had total control of it, for the *Housmans Peace Diary*. And so I designed and produced that [in] 1984, the first one.

In 1985, 5 Cally Road helped a new business get going over the road. When a lingerie shop over the road closed down, the building's owner, local landlord Mr Stuckey, offered to lease them the shop. Nigel suggested opening a wholefood shop, Sandy put together a business plan, *Peace News* Trustees lent them money to get going and Mr Stuckey typed them up a one-page lease on his typewriter. Opposite 5 Cally Road, Peacemeal Wholefoods began.

Sandy, along with Paul Robinson, opened and ran the shop, selling vegetarian food. Sandy explained:

It was fairly successful from the start. And we developed takeaway foods which there was a great demand for. There was very little other decent food available at King's Cross at the time, it was pretty dire. And so, we quite quickly built up a large takeaway business and the other followed in its wake sort of thing. So, there was me and Paul working there, and quite a lot of Paul's friends worked there ... and most of them were in or associated with this punk group called Karma Sutra. And, we also had various people from other [punk] groups, some people from Flux of Pink Indians put some shelves up for us, and Pete from Crass did odd jobs for us, with the electrics and things.

Peacemeal Wholefoods, a week after it opened in 1985

RIGHT: Housmans and Peace News stalls at Glastonbury, 1982

LEFT: Peacemeal Wholefoods, a week after it opened in 1985

Steve Craftman, who volunteered at Switchboard between 1979 and 1987 remembered they had a meals allowance for Switchboard volunteers, which was 'the price of something healthy from over the road'.

Housmans took bookstalls to pacifist events, radical bookfairs, Pride marches, music festivals and gigs. From the humble beginning of their first Glastonbury bookstall, at which they made £250, the stalls became increasingly important. In 1990 stalls at Glastonbury and Pride together raised £3,500, which was a significant contribution to the shop's income.[10] In 1984 Housmans helped to organise the first Anarchist Bookfair in London, along with A Distribution, the Anarchist Book Service and Freedom Bookshop.[11] Peacemeal occasionally took to the road too, even providing refreshments on a train specially chartered in 1988 to take people from London to Manchester to protest Section 28.[12]

10   Housmans Board, 'Minutes of Housmans Board Meeting 4 July 1990', 1990, Housmans Archive, Housmans Minute Book 1990–95.

11   'History' <http://anarchistbookfair.org.uk/history.html> [accessed 21 June 2022].

12   Clause 28 of the Local Government Act came into force

in 1988, making it illegal for local authorities to 'promote' homosexuality and banned schools from teaching the 'acceptability of homosexuality as a pretended family relationship'. A massive demonstration was held in Manchester on 20 February 1988 to oppose it, just before it was enacted into law in May 1988.

During the miners' strike from 1984 to 1985 there was a collection tin on the bookshop counter to raise money for the strikers. Mark Ashton, who co-founded Lesbians and Gays Support the Miners with Mike Jackson, worked occasionally in the bookshop as well as at London Gay Switchboard upstairs, and Housmans provided a bookstall at the now iconic Lesbians and Gays Support the Miners benefit concert, Pits and Perverts. The concert attracted 1,400 people to see Bronski Beat perform at the Electric Ballroom in Camden, raising £5,000 for the miners.[13]

Bookshop customers, Rosie remembered, tended to be:

people [who] were very involved in peace movement things, ... people involved with anarchist things. People that were obviously in left groups, organised type of groups, would also come, because we sold loads of newspapers and magazines and all that kind of thing. Not as many women came, to be frank, because there were a lot of other [feminist] shops and they did much more for women. Although women came in, I would

13    'Bronski Bash Nets £5,000 for Miners', *Capital Gay*, 14 December 1984, 172 edition.

Housmans at Glastonbury, 1982

say the clientele was more men. And then obviously because Lesbian and Gay Switchboard was upstairs, and some of the staff were gay, there was quite a lot of gay men, more so than lesbians....

You'd get an occasional person who maybe had just wandered in, didn't know what it was, but most people came in because they knew it was there. Some of them would have been people that were going to other parts of the building, but some of them were ones that had sought it out because they knew about it. But then, against that, there would be the completely office type people that would come in [for stationery], get their stuff and then just came out again.

**Nigel remembered their best customer as a woman he suspected worked for MI5, who would visit once a fortnight to buy a copy of every magazine they stocked.**

**In 1984 Rosie left Housmans after two years to take up a job in another bookshop, Centerprise, a few miles away in Hackney, east London. She felt Centerprise was more aligned with her politics at the time. In comparison, she said Housmans was part of a:**

very abstract, esoteric form of kind of activism. I'm not saying it wasn't real-life stuff, and it was, but I was much more interested in ... stuff that's really linked to local communities, that really benefits local people. I mean Housmans could have been anywhere, it really didn't engage with the local community, apart from selling it stationery, and that was a bit of a marginal thing. It didn't really reflect the local community.... I think [what] I felt about Housmans, was [that] it was a kind of political project that happened to be in that shop because [that was where it] ... was purchased.

**However, there were communities in King's Cross who made use of Housmans and Peacemeal. While many long-established businesses in King's Cross began to close down due to redevelopment plans making the area's future uncertain, there were increasing numbers of squatters, punks and LGBTQ+ people in the area. These were the sort of people who liked radical bookshops, although they might not have had much money to spend. The bookshop was not just somewhere to buy things, it was**

a centre of information. You could pick up a leaflet or a free paper and browse the noticeboard to find a flatmate or get news of events.

Clifford Williams came to the bookshop in the late 1970s and early 1980s. At the time, he had friends who were squatting in King's Cross. He'd buy badges, pick up out-of-date copies of *Peace News* for free and take them back to the squat and find out about gay events. Clifford was familiar with Housmans already as his father, Frank Williams, was a Quaker and peace activist who worked in the bookshop at the time. He said:

> If you walk in as a punk to W H Smith's, they might keep a very close eye on you, or they might ask you to leave. But if you go into Housmans, I felt, oh, this is a place I can feel at home, because my dad helps here … and they've got all this peace literature and all this stuff that I'm familiar with. And there's always good stuff to browse. So, I was perfectly comfortable to be in Housmans.

Sandy Donaldson described what King's Cross was like when Peacemeal was open:

> We had Rough Trade Records and distribution move in the area. And there was also Better Badges, and Copyart, which was an early community type thing, and Zed Books, and there was Scala cinema. So, this was the sort of mix of a lot of our clientele. At some stage we got a drinks licence so we could start selling organic wine and things as well. I think our first customer for the wine was Shane MacGowan of the Pogues …
>
> There was a lot going on [in King's Cross]. There were lots of clubs and things. There [were LGBTQ+ venues like] the Bell pub … and there was the Prince Albert. There was a sort of garage down the back of us which Mr Stucky also owned, and it used to be the Caledonian coach station or something. And it was … empty, and at some stage he let the Mutoid Waste Company move in for a time, and they put some shows on there. So [people were] queuing down the side of the shop to get into this show in the evening. Yes, it felt quite a happening area with things going on.

## A Movement Bookshop

While radical bookshops were thriving around the country, some of the people involved in Housmans had very different ideas about what kind of 'movement' bookshop they should be. Jim Huggon, who worked at Housmans from 1969 to 1982, worried the shop was focusing less on peace and nonviolence, which he thought should be the priority, and becoming 'far more gay and feminist and the rest of it'.

Rosie Ilett, who started work in 1982, the same year Jim left, thought differently. She explained that Housmans chose not to focus much on feminism as:

> We were only about a mile away from Sisterwrite in Islington, so we sort of knew ... commercially there's no point in building up a massive feminist section of a bookshop when there's one down the road.

In 1979 a specialist LGBTQ+ bookshop, Gay's the Word, also opened not far from Housmans in Bloomsbury. Despite having a specialist shop nearby, Housmans continued to stock LGBTQ+ books, as it had since at least the early 1970s, as Julian Hows, member of the GLF and Switchboard, remembered:

This sort of grungy building, with some people who were involved with GLF serving behind the counter ... in sort of thick Marxist-Leninist sweaters, with holes in, and a bit grubby. But it was the only place where you could see and find things like radical gay press from other countries. ... And, being a schoolkid with not much money, what was interesting is that you could [read] it in the back of the Housmans bookshop, and [the] staff didn't really mind, so long as ... you didn't make it too grubby or too curly-edged. So that for me was a bit like having a radical gay library on the doorstep.

It was not easy to find LGBTQ+ books in the 1970s and early 1980s. Not many bookshops stocked them, and those that did mainly had to import them as most were published in the USA. An archaic law, the Customs Consolidation Act 1876, meant that LGBTQ+ books could be seized by Customs and Excise on entry to the UK. On 10 April 1984, Gay's the Word bookshop (along with the homes of some of its directors) was raided by Customs and Excise officers, who confiscated thousands of books as part of 'Operation Tiger.' Over the next two years thousands more LGBTQ+ books would be confiscated by Customs, including titles by Gore Vidal and Jean-Paul Sartre.[14]

In February 1984, Sandy Donaldson had ordered some books for Housmans from Giovanni's Room, an LGBTQ+ bookshop in Philadelphia.[15] The books never arrived, and shortly afterwards, a note from Customs confirmed the books had been confiscated on grounds of obscenity.

Sandy said the Housmans board chose not to dispute the confiscation of the books:

The board of Housmans didn't want to get involved in another court case. They didn't see it as being central to their mission. And they had only just got out of another court case.

This, Sandy said, was disappointing for the staff:

But knowing that they were only just getting over this other legal case, and knowing the sort of financial positions they were in, you didn't really feel it was something you could push them on.

Meanwhile, over 140 titles (amounting to thousands of books) had been seized from Gay's the Word in three actions by Customs between April and October 1984. Then, on 21 November 1984, eight directors of Gay's the Word and the manager were

---

14    Graham McKerrow, 'Saving Gay's the Word: The Campaign to Protect a Bookshop and the Right to Import Queer Literature', in *Queer Between the Covers*, ed. by Leila Kassir and Richard Espley, Histories of Queer Publishing and Publishing Queer Voices (University of London Press, 2021), pp. 91–123. <https://www.jstor.org/stable/j.ctv123x59r.11> [accessed 28 September 2022].

15    'Letter to Mr Donaldson from Ed Hermance', 1984, Bishopsgate Institute, 5 Cally Road Archive.

charged with multiple counts of conspiring to import indecent and obscene material. They were supported by the Defend Gay's the Word campaign, which began after the first raid, and a defence fund, which raised over £55,000.[16] The nine defendants would ultimately face 100 charges. Their trial at the Old Bailey was scheduled for October 1986. Luckily, a few months before the trial was set to take place, a different case about the importation of sex dolls from Germany was won on the grounds that the dolls would not be illegal if made in the UK, and with this precedent the charges were dropped, and the books returned.[17]

Rosie said the bookshop staff took 'a libertarian sort of view that, it was really important not to censor things'. Housmans was somewhere you could find material that even other radical bookshops might not have sold, including *On Our Backs*, a 'pro-sex' lesbian magazine published in San Franciso from 1984, which was opposed by the 'anti-porn' strand of the feminist movement because it featured S&M erotica. Switchboard volunteer Diana James remembered *On Our Backs* being the subject of a protest outside Housmans:

> And so, some of these feminists were standing outside with placards and stuff, and shouting at everybody that went in the door, about them stocking *On Our Backs*. So, that was kind of fun. I would sort of stand in the door waving my copy at them. Which really got them stirred up. I couldn't resist, it was like, nobody tells me what I can and can't read, that's what feminism is supposed to be about.

When Harry Mister retired, the board seem to have worried that the pacifist focus of the shop might be lost. They wrote a statement of staff and board responsibility in April 1982, which reminded the workers that the bookshop's key aim was 'the building of a pacifist society based on nonviolent means of resolving social and international conflicts'.[18] At one meeting the shop staff attempted to reassure the board that 'they all wished to make clear their overall commitment to the pacifist role of the shop. Even if they were not all personally pacifists, they were all anti-militarists.'[19]

However, minutes of board meetings record that the board were often worried about some of the literature being distributed through the bookshop. Ramsey Kanaan recalled one particular disagreement between the board and Housmans staff:

> In the early eighties there was this paper called *Class War* ... done by these anarchists who deliberately kind of copied the tabloid style. So lurid headlines, grizzly photographs ... the paper was a phenomenal seller, like it caught on really quickly, it was incredibly

16  'Defend Gay's The Word Campaign Archive', Bishopsgate Institute <https://www.bishopsgate.org.uk/collections/defend-gays-the-word-campaign-archive> [accessed 28 September 2022].

17  McKerrow

18  Housmans Board, 'A Statement of the Board's Responsibilities in Relation to the Staff, and the Staff's Responsibilities in Relation to the Board', 1982, Housmans Archive, Housmans Minute Book 1972–83.

19  Board meeting, 19 Feb 1982.

popular... So Housmans would sell several hundred copies of each issue of *Class War*, it was their bestselling paper, you know, outsold everything else, whether anarchist or Trotskyist or you name it ... The trustees went apoplectic because *Class War* not only copied that tabloid style, but revelled in it. So, they had pictures of cops being violently assaulted or cops covered in blood. Each week instead of the Page 3 pin-up from *The Sun* ... their pin-up was of like a badly beaten policeman ... And they had like pictures of Margaret Thatcher with her head chopped off and all that kind of shit. So the *Peace News* Trustees went apoplectic at a certain point and said, you can't stock *Class War* anymore because, you know [it's] against what we believe in, or whatever the fuck. And the five [shop staff] said, if we can't stock *Class War* we're resigning en masse. And so the trustees had to back down and they carried on selling *Class War*. But again, to me that was just another fantastic example of the genuine non-sectarian-ness of the people that worked there. You know, perhaps only Malcolm of the five of them actually thought that *Class War* was really good or agreed with its politics, shall we say. But the other four, who were probably almost as aghast, to varying degrees, as the trustees, backed that concept of non-sectarian distribution of information on the Left 100 per cent.

On 10 May 1993, the *Daily Star* reported that Housmans sold *An Phoblacht*, Sinn Fein's newspaper. This prompted a discussion at the Housmans board meeting over 'whether it was appropriate for a pacifist bookshop such as Housmans to sell a paper which manifestly gave enthusiastic and uncritical support to the IRA'. Housmans workers felt 'it right to make available minority papers that were not easily obtainable elsewhere so that interested people could make informed judgements'. The board, while not approving, did not overrule them.[20]

20   'Minutes of Board and Staff Meeting on Tuesday 18
     May 1993', Housmans Archive, Housmans Minute Book
     1990–95.

# peace news

## for nonviolent revolution

No. 2067 Friday 7 April 1978                    Fortnightly  Price 15p

# SAVE US FROM SILENCE!

**pull-out poster inside**

5 Caledonian Road, Kings Cross, London N1.

Tel: 01-278 1976

Wednesday, 20 November 1974

## SUPPORTERS' NEWSLETTER 1

Dear friends,

This is the first of what we intend to be a regular series of newsletters to supporters of CAAT. After the next one, they should be produced at about 6-weekly intervals, to fit in with the timetable of Campaign Council meetings, and with the work of other committees.

During the past week, the Campaign has started to make itself felt in the outside world. A press release was widely distributed at the beginning of last week, and as a result a few presspeople turned up at a press conference on Thursday 14th, in - I don't Fleet Street. Speaking at the conference was Frank Allaun MP, and several people from the Campaign. Another press statement was issued after the conference, and the final result was quite a large piece on the back page of the Guardian, and another sympathetic piece in the Morning Star. If in fact you've found any other coverage, or come across anything of interest in any publication, please send them in to the Campaign as an attempt to build up as much background material as possible.

Some points from the press statements before and after the press conference:

"This Campaign is a project set up and sponsored by 8 peace movement organisations, and has several initial aims -

- A comprehensive educational and informational campaign on the subject, introducing and questioning the arms trade amongst the general public.
- The raising of the arms trade in the "political arena", and its implications.
- In order to start with an achievable objective, the concentration on exports from Britain, and more specifically on arms sales by one particular corporation...."

"... At today's inaugural press conference, this corporation was named as EMI. The amount of armaments-related work done by EMI is substantial, and yet is only a minority of the work done by the Company. This therefore means that their changing over from production for war to production for peace would be relatively easy compared to many companies; and they thus will provide a useful example to others when they do in fact stop. Also, their interests in so many everyday products gives scope for a wide range of action by supporters of this Campaign in case discussion alone does not change their policy...."

Other items of news relevant to the launching of the Campaign will be apparent from the top of this page. We now have an office and phone number! The office is a room in the Peace News/Housmans Bookshop building. After quite some work on clearing out the historic debris of previous peace movement occupants, the room now has CAAT-type posters up and is sparsely furnished. What is much needed now is for someone to drop in with a typewriter that they don't need; and also someone with a filing cabinet... For the time being, storage space is cramped, and typewriters have to be borrowed from fellow inhabitants of the building, when they're available.

5, CALEDONIAN ROAD, KINGS CROSS, LONDON N1 9DX

(01- 278 1976)

Friday 27 December 1974

## NEWSLETTER 2

Dear Friends,

Firstly, an apology to any of you who received your first newsletter either very late, or a little singed, or - worst of all - not at all. Within 10 minutes of the major batch of newsletter 1 being posted, the pillar box containing them blew up (it was the box right outside our office here, and the first of the three to blow up that Monday night). It was known more or less which ones were there, and so those which couldn't be salvaged were sent out again. We hope you all got one in the end.

Since that previous newsletter, our mailing list has doubled, and also copies are being sent out by other organisations - so we're starting with 500 copies of this, and hoping to need more before - the next one in six weeks' time. So, support and interest is growing - things don't look too bad after only about six weeks - but a lot more has to happen before we can make much impact. The rest of this newsletter tells you of some things that are happening, and many more that could happen if our supporters (that's you) are prepared to help.

Apart from the issue of the arms trade being raised at a number of conferences, as appropriate, there are some meetings being arranged by some local groups already.

In Bristol, there is a meeting at Redland College on Thursday 9 January with a speaker about CAAT, organised by the World Development Movement; a meeting to launch a local CAAT group at Horfields Friends Meeting House on Thursday 16 January; and a speaker about Britain and the arms trade at the area FOR Conference on 22 February; further details on these from Frank Rix, 75 Kinsale Road, Knowle, Bristol.

In Leeds, a meeting is being arranged for early in February about CAAT.

In London, the London School of Nonviolence is having speakers about the arms trade at its meetings on 3 and 5 February in the Crypt of St-Martin-in-the-Fields Church, Trafalgar Square; 7pm.

A meeting is being arranged at Harpenden during the spring.

There are many areas of the country with several people interested in CAAT, but who perhaps don't know of one another. So could you please write in to volunteer to be a local contact for your area - you will then be sent the names of others near you who have been in touch with the Campaign. If we are to have an impact, it's very important to have groups all over the place, so please be in touch as soon as possible.

There are many things that local groups - and individuals - can be doing, there were lots of suggestions in the first newsletter. More suggestions include the production of an exhibition on this topic, something mobile. We've already had a request to mount a display, but as yet we have nothing appropriate. Could your group help? Then we needn't turn down further chances!

Also, you could volunteer to help with the working groups in London who are "servicing" the Campaign. For example, could you help the research group? They need more volunteers who could spend time in libraries digging up useful facts and figures for the factsheets they want to produce.

Sponsor: Campaign for Nuclear Disarmament, Fellowship of Reconciliation, Friends Peace, and International Relations Committee, London School of Nonviolence, Pax Christi, Peace Pledge Union, Women's International League for Peace and Freedom.

mediate acceptance
month.

Contact by Mail.

CANDIDATES NAME .Mick Jackson.

DATE .24./.4./.83.

INTERVIEWER .Mark Holden.

TRAINER .Kevin Mc

If the candidate has answered 'yes' to question 'B' on the application
form, i.e. if the candidate has been interviewed before, please study
the previous forms and make notes below.

COMMENTS

...terview — Better than I thought it would be
danger in orgs like S/O. — individuals
can be terribly efficious — could get off on
own prestige. Avoid trap of seeing yourself
as a latter-day Florence Nightingale.

...stions? — gay

Will s/he be free Sundays? Yes.

**Shifts/ Frequency** not more than once a fortnight. ☐
variable — yes. — eves & weekends.

**Which Group?** had exper. in most groups ☐
minimum 5 hours.

**Relevant Religious Views** agnostic.   M.C.C. Quest.   G.C.M with prompt.
Quakers. J.G.C.
re religion — oppressive, patriarchal — would offer & suggest.

**Relevant Political Views** NF — they've got to be fought.
**esp. Racism/ Fascism** C.P. allright.          Don't believe youth
& capitalism could exist.
for gay rights — Labour. G.L.C. —
Liberals mean nice things — don't know what
they'd be like in practice.
Blacks — Racist view — not take info.

**Hoax/ (Abuse)/ (Silent Calls)** — telewankers — sympathetic (tough).
maybe a ♀.
explain don't think they're phoning for genuine reasons,
maybe gay & fucked up about it — or anti gay. ask if gay.

**Teenage Callers** G.Y.M. / L.G.T.G / y. lesbian Group (prompt).
gay video project.
le — Local S/B & encourage re-call to London & G.Y.M.

— Movements / Mutilations / Carried Red hior.

3d **TV /TS Scene** "Someone who cares to wear clothes of
opp sex" ♀ too.

Porchester Hall) "Someone who has actually changed sex"
or want to.
- Kent / **SE Geography** Balts — Trafalgar — night bus. green lanes.
Section.
- N.E. Colehern — Heaven — Tube. district.
- West Earls court — Meathras — picadilly. All bus.
Clapham — East / Roehampton SW / Harrow Msex N.N.
Croydon — steamer B.R.
station — victoria.

**Sexual Techniques/** first fuckee — do you want
Abs/ **V.D. Knowledge/ Attitudes** to be fucked.
- gonorrea ✓ N J V V K.Y. jelly. — or other lubricant
anal warts & vaseline — don't think it's good. Many.
penis? — fucker be gentle — relax.
1 st. S/M — up to individuals —
ris — in vagina. FF — put my hand inside arse.
first sex — what do you 7A how to do it — very careful.
want to do be clean stop if
don't feel pressured. its not nails — take
enjoy yourself. use palm there might off jewellers.

Under the following TWO headings the interviewer should list the positive and negative qualities of the candidate. Notes about interest level, Gay awareness and advice to traier or reason for rejection should also be made here.

POSITIVE POINTS

everything except
below.

NEGATIVE POINTS

South London Ents.
teenage Groups — in tandem.

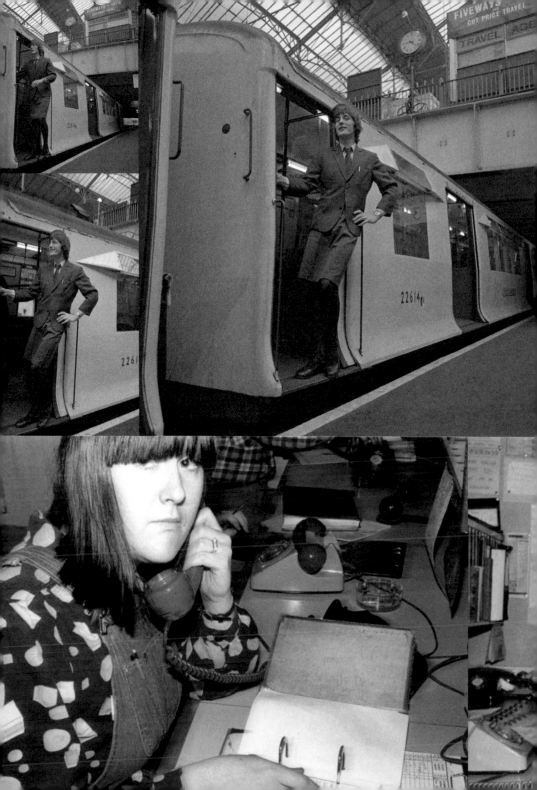

Hello Housmans people!

enclosed are 20 copies of Catalyst which is just out, thanks again for the help in distribution,

i'll get in touch again when i've got a definate date for the Exeter Cross gig — April 27th. looks certain, but it hasn't been confirmed, i really hope you can make it,

See you soon,

lots of love + anarchy,

RICH.

xxx.

HOUSMANS
THE
RADICAL
BOOKSHOP

Housmans...
PUBLISHERS · BOOKSELLERS · STATIONERS

8 May 1984

Dear Mr. Donaldson,

I'm sorry to hear you haven't received the books invoiced on Hous.-1 (or 3387/8) sent 4 Feb. '84. Today we put a trace on it at the post office. I can't hold out much hope for the trace doing any good. If customs seizes it, we will get back a copy of the notice of seizure sent to the recipient — we did send the box to Nigel Kemp, by the way. I don't think customs may seize goods without sending a notice of seizure to the recipient, so Nigel should certainly have received the notice by now if the goods were seized.

Our experience has been that goods take 4 to 6 weeks to get from Philadelphia to London, so, yes, the goods are long overdue.

As a pre precaution we've not put "Giovanni's Room" on the outside of the package to the U.K. for two to three months. Because 4 Feb. is slightly longer than three months, "Giovanni's Room" may have appeared on the package. I'll certainly let you know if we hear from the post office.

Best wishes,
Ed Hermance

RAINFOREST

COOPERATIVELY PRODUCED RIO (BRAZIL) AND ARE 100% COTTON

£6.75

ACCESS VISA

Housmans Bookshop
Kings Cross

FESTIVAL EYE

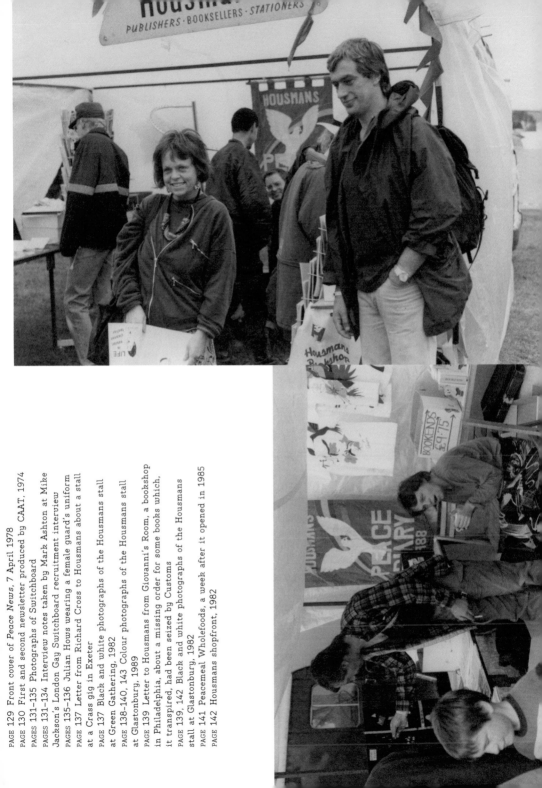

Everything they don't
want you to know.

McDollars™ McGreedy™ McCancer™ McMurder™ McDisease™ McProfits™ McDeadly™ McHunger™

THIS LEAFLET is asking you to think for a moment about what lies behind McDonald's clean, bright image. It's got a lot to hide.

"At McDonald's we've got time for you" goes the jingle. Why then do they

FIFTY ACRES EVERY MINUTE
EVERY year an area of rainforest the size of Britain is cut down or defoliated, and burnt.

• What's so unhealthy about McDonald's

# CHAPTER 7

# INCURABLE OPTIMISM

From 1987, the future of 5 Cally Road became increasingly uncertain. First, plans for a new railway development threatened to demolish the entire local area, which suffered from planning blight as a result. The local community got together to campaign vigorously against the plans. Partly due to the threatened development, Housmans entered its most serious financial crisis.

In this same period one of the building's tenants, London Greenpeace, campaigned against the McDonald's corporation. The global fast-food chain issued libel proceedings against five members of London Greenpeace to try to stop them handing out leaflets outside their restaurants. 5 Cally Road was one of the places used to support two of these people, Helen Steel and Dave Morris, as they took on McDonald's in what would become England's longest ever trial.

### London Greenpeace

London Greenpeace formed in 1971 to combine environmental campaigning with anti-militarism (see Chapter 2). By the 1980s they were also increasingly concerning themselves with social justice, animal rights and anti-capitalism.

In 1983 and 1984 they had initiated and helped coordinate a series of anti-capitalist demonstrations called 'Stop the City,' which were described as a carnival against war, oppression and exploitation. At the first event on 29 September 1983, over a thousand demonstrators brought the city of London to a standstill. Many of the demonstrators were young punks; Penny Rimbaud from Crass described the day as 'the best gig of the year'.[1] With its decentralised organisation that encouraged autonomous affinity group actions and willingness to knit together a wide range of issues and groups at once, Stop the City was a forerunner of Reclaim the Streets and the anti-globalisation movement that took off in the late 1990s.

After Stop the City, London Greenpeace attracted a younger generation of activists who were often interested in anarchism and animal rights. One young animal rights activist, Paul Gravett, joined London Greenpeace in 1986. He first came along to a public meeting to hear a guest speaker from the Animal Liberation Front and remembered visiting the group's office in 5 Cally Road shortly afterwards.

When Paul joined, the group had started a campaign against McDonald's. They launched a day of action against the company, the International Day of Action Against

Protesters celebrate at Stop the City on 29 September 1983

---

1    Rich Cross, '"There Is No Authority But Yourself": The Individual and the Collective in British Anarcho-Punk', *Music and Politics*, IV.2 (2010) <https://doi.org/10.3998/mp.9460447.0004.203>.

McDonald's, in 1985. Paul said that he was 'very enthusiastic' about the campaign:

I was by then a vegan, I had been doing animal rights for a few years. And what I liked about [the campaign] was the way it attacked McDonald's from all sorts of angles. It was a very broad-based campaign, so it looked at environmental, health, workers' rights issues, as well as the killing of animals. And it became a very successful and popular campaign. I don't know, it sort of caught the mood of the times in a way ... some campaigns do. And, we being the sort of libertarian group London Greenpeace was, we didn't want to organise and tell everyone what to do; we wanted groups to get on and do their own thing. And they did. And there were lots of groups ... environmental, animal rights groups, anarchist groups, who started demonstrating, campaigning against their own local McDonald's. Because of course, there were McDonald's all over the place. And it wasn't just in this country either, it was like, throughout the world, we used to get letters about the campaigns and things. And ... [they] produced a fact sheet called ... *What's*

*Wrong With McDonald's? Everything they don't want you to know.* And it was a fold-out leaflet, quite big, lots of text and lots of information. I think that got printed in about 1986, quite quickly after I was really involved in the group.

**In the autumn of 1990, five members of London Greenpeace were served writs for libel by the McDonald's corporation. Paul was one of the five served. He said:**

Actually, none of the five of us who were sued had actually ... written it, or had a major role in producing the fact sheet. But we were nonetheless sued because ... they said we were responsible for its distribution.

Paul Gravett reading *Peace News*, 1983

# What's wrong with McDonald's?

## Everything they don't want you to know.

THIS LEAFLET is asking you to think for a moment about what lies behind McDonald's clean, bright image. It's got a lot to hide.

*"At McDonald's we've got time for you"* goes the jingle. But why then do they design the service so that you're in and out as soon as possible? Why is it so difficult to relax in a McDonald's? Why do you feel hungry again so soon after eating a Big Mac?

We're all subject to the pressures of stupid advertising, consumerist hype, and the fast pace of big city life — but it doesn't take any special intelligence to start asking questions about McDonald's and to realise that something is seriously wrong.

The more you find out about McDonald's processed food, the less attractive it becomes, as this leaflet will show. The truth about hamburgers is enough to put you off them for life.

- ## What's the connection between McDonald's and starvation in the 'Third World'?

THERE's no point feeling *guilty* about eating while watching starving African children on T.V. If you do send money to Band Aid, or shop at Oxfam, etc., that's morally good but politically useless. It shifts the blame from governments and does nothing to challenge the power of multinational corporations.

**HUNGRY FOR DOLLARS**

- McDonald's is one of several giant corporations with investments in vast tracts of land in poor countries, sold to them by the dollar-hungry rulers (often military) and privileged elites, evicting the small farmers that live there growing food for their own people.

The power of the US dollar means that in order to buy technology and manufactured goods, poor countries are trapped into producing more and more food for export to the States. *Out of 40 of the world's poorest countries, 36 export food to the USA — the wealthiest.*

**ECONOMIC IMPERIALISM**

- Some 'Third World' countries, where most

*A typical image of 'Third World' poverty — the kind often used by charities to get compassion and money. This diverts attention from one cause: exploitation by multinationals like McDonald's.*

countries are being used for our benefit — for tea, coffee, tobacco, etc. — while people there are *starving*, McDonald's is directly involved in this economic imperialism, which keeps most black people poor and hungry while many whites grow fat.

**GROSS MISUSE OF RESOURCES**

GRAIN is fed to cattle in South American countries to produce the meat in McDonald's hamburgers. Cattle consume 10 times the amount of grain and soy that humans do: one calorie of beef demands ten calories of grain. Of the 145 million tons of grain and soy fed to livestock, only 21 million tons of meat and by-products are used. *The waste is 124 million*

### FIFTY ACRES EVERY MINUTE

EVERY year an area of rainforest the size of Britain is cut down or defoliated, and burnt. Globally, one billion people depend on water flowing from these forests, which soak up rain and release it gradually. The disaster in Eth **and** release it gradually. The disaster in Ethiopia and Sudan is at least partly due to un- controlled deforestation in Amazonia — where there are now about 100,000 beef ranches — torrential rains sweep down through the tree- less valleys. T.V. appeals for the drought sun, become useless for agriculture. It has been estimated that this destruction causes at least one species of animal, plant or insect to become extinct every few hours.

- ## What's so unhealthy about McDonald's food?

McDONALD's try to show in their "Nutrition Guide" (which is full of impressive-looking but really quite irrelevant facts & figures) that mass-produced hamburgers, chips, colas, milkshakes, etc., are a useful and nutritious part of any diet.

What they don't make clear is that a diet high in fat, sugar, animal products and salt (sodium), and low in fibre, vitamins and minerals — which describes an average McDonald's meal — is linked with cancers of the breast and bowel, and heart disease. This is accepted medical fact, not a cranky theory. Every year in Britain, heart disease alone causes about 180,000 deaths.

**FAST = JUNK**

- Even if they like eating them, most people recognise that processed burgers and synthetic chips, served up in paper and plastic containers, is junk-food. McDonald's prefer the name "fast-food". This is not just because it is manufactured and served up as quickly as possible — it has to be *eaten* quickly too. It's a sign of the junk-quality of Big Macs that people actually hold competitions to see who can eat one in the shortest time.

**PAYING FOR THE HABIT**

- Chewing is essential for good health, as it promotes the flow of digestive juices which break down the food and send nutrients into the blood. McDonald's food is so lacking in bulk it is hardly possible to chew it. Even their own figures show that a "quarter-pounder" is 48% water. This sort of fake food encourages over-eating, and the high sugar and sodium content can make people develop a kind of addiction — a 'craving'. That means more profit for McDonald's, but constipation, clogged arteries and heart attacks for many customers.

- ## Why is it wrong for McDonald's to destroy rainforests?

AROUND the Equator there is a lush green belt of incredibly beautiful tropical forest, untouched by human development for one hundred million years, supporting about half of all Earth's life-forms, including some 30,000 plant species, and producing a major part of the planet's crucial supply of oxygen.

**PET FOOD & LITTER**

- McDonald's and Burger King are two of the many US corporations using lethal poisons to destroy vast areas of Central American rainforest to create grazing pastures for cattle to be sent back to the States as burgers and to provide fast-food packaging materials. (Don't be fooled by McDonald's saying they use recycled paper; only a tiny per cent of it is. The truth is it takes 800 *square miles* of forest just to keep them supplied with paper for one year. Tons of this end up littering the cities of 'developed' countries).

**COLONIAL INVASION**

- Not only are McDonald's and many other corporations contributing to a major ecological catastrophe, they are forcing the tribal peoples in the rainforests of their ancestral territories where they have lived peacefully without damaging their environment for thousands of years. This is a typical example of the arrogance and viciousness

IF THE SLAUGHTERHOUSE DOESN'T GET YOU

The five activists investigated their legal options, using their two hours of free legal aid, which is all it was possible to get for a libel case. It did not look promising; unlike in criminal trials, where defendants are innocent until proven guilty, the onus was on the defendants to actively prove that all the statements made in the leaflet were true. McDonald's had already used its almost endless reserves of money to threaten libel cases against any organisation or media outlet that publicly criticised the company, and fifty of these organisations had already apologised rather than go to court.[2]

Three of the group, Paul included, reluctantly decided to apologise, but two of them, Helen Steel and Dave Morris, refused. In the *McLibel* documentary about the court case, Helen Steel said:

> It just really stuck in the throat to apologise to McDonald's. I thought it was them that should have been apologising to us — well not us specifically, but to society for the damage they do to society and the environment.[3]

## King's Cross Railway Lands

While London Greenpeace were campaigning against McDonald's, in 1987 British Rail launched a plan to develop the King's Cross Railway Lands, a derelict former goods yard to the north of the station.[4] Although no one knew it at the time, this plan threatened not only 5 Cally Road, but the future of the entire surrounding area. Diana Shelley described what happened:

> So, the King's Cross Railway Lands had obviously been a prime site for people to think of redeveloping for I don't know how long, because you didn't really need potato sheds any more, and things like that. And, you know, there it is, sat in the middle of London, and it's big, and it even had some nice buildings, and current developers have very graciously left a couple of them for us ... And, in 1987 something called the London Regeneration Consortium sort of stepped forward to say, 'Yes, we're going to redevelop it.' And the King's Cross Railway Lands Group ... was set up basically to try and do what you have to do with property developers, if at all possible, and Phil [Jeffries] got involved in that ... They had an exhibition [showing] the wonderful brave new world that was going to be developed and I was with Phil, and he went, 'What's that line running across the map?' Well that line was just a proposal for the Channel Tunnel rail link that they hadn't bothered to mention.

2   Rob Evans and Paul Lewis, *The True Story of Britain's Secret Police* (London: Guardian, 2014).

3   *McLibel: Full Documentary (Official)*, dir. by Spanner Films, 2015 <https://www.youtube.com/watch?v=V58kK4r26yk> [accessed 14 July 2022].

4   'Railway Threat, Blight and Survival', in *King's Cross: A Sense of Place*, by Angela Inglis and Nigel Buckner (Leicester: Matador, 2012).

Phil's keen eye for detail had uncovered a key part of the plan that British Rail was keeping quiet: they wanted to combine this development with a new high-speed railway that would link north London with the Channel Tunnel. At the time the Channel Tunnel was being built, with Waterloo as the terminus, and was due to open in 1994. The station for the high-speed train would not, however, be built on the vacant Railway Lands, but rather the 'low-level station' British Rail envisaged would be located beneath the station and the streets to its east and south. This would mean demolishing 150 buildings, including eighty-eight homes and 168 shops, amongst them 5 Cally Road.[5] Diana Shelley described the plans as 'quite the most

5    'Railway Threat, Blight and Survival'.
6    'Railway Threat, Blight and Survival'.

7    'Housmans Minute Book 1990–95', Housmans Archive.

extraordinary piece of railway construction mismanagement that you could imagine'.

The local community realised the full implications of British Rail's plans in December 1987, when they were finally made public. Phil Jeffries at the time lived in the flat at the top of 5 Cally Road. He was Diana Shelley's partner and a founding member and chair of the King's Cross Railway Lands Group, which campaigned against the destruction of the neighbourhood by British Rail's plans. He was the main link, Diana said, between the building and the wider campaign.

Randal Keynes, writing in Angela Inglis's King's Cross: A Sense of Place describes how, to compulsorily purchase the buildings they wanted to demolish, British Rail needed to get a private bill through Parliament.[6] This meant local people could petition Parliament to make their case, but first they needed to learn the procedures for doing so, as Diana explained:

> Parliamentary petitioning is like swearing an affidavit, and it costs. For the King's Cross Bill, it only cost two quid a petition. ... But, the whole process of getting petitions [is] you get them agreed, the person signs it, ... you have legal advice. The way it was done was, you set up a workshop and people come through and they pay their £2, and there were 282 petitions lodged against the King's Cross Bill. And then they went to some, I think a Court of Referees, which I do remember going to a very boring session of with Phil, where people had to argue what their *locus standi* was as petitioners. You know, were they near enough to be affected, and things like that. And only 151 were accepted, but that's still quite a big total.

The Bill was deposited on 29 November 1988 and went through several stages of scrutiny. After it was debated for the first time it went to a Committee of MPs to be considered. At this stage the campaigners had a chance to give evidence to the Committee and present their findings. Phil Jeffries had examined British Rail's plans for engineering failings and found importantly that the proposed platforms were too short for the trains.

The Committee heard 51 days of evidence before it could report. It concluded that it had to approve the bill but only if British Rail came up with a different route and show how it would be financed by the time it got to the Lords. It took sixteen months for British Rail to develop the new route, which would approach King's Cross from the east, and the process of reading and debate in Parliament continued. *Peace News* Trustees and Housmans submitted petitions at various stages of the process, with Phil Jeffries acting as Housmans' agent for their petition to the House of Lords in 1992.[7]

Meanwhile the area's planning blight got worse, due to the uncertainty caused by the railway link plan. As more shops and houses became empty, the area became well known for street-based drug-dealing and sex work. The area had its own special unit of the Metropolitan Police, Operation Welwyn. King's Cross was splashed all over the news when, in October 1991, the Director of Public Prosecutions, Allan Green, was arrested for kerb-crawling in Goods Way.[8]

The residents' persistence in campaigning as the Bill made its way through Parliament meant that British Rail were forced to show how they would make the rail link affordable. Eventually, a cheaper option proposed by Union Railways, of basing the rail link at St Pancras, above rather than underground, was chosen by the government: meaning the homes and businesses at the bottom of Cally Road were saved. On 24 January 1994 the King's Cross Railways Bill was withdrawn.[9]

## Housmans Struggles On

Housmans had, like other local businesses, suffered from the area's decline. As the 1990s began, the bookshop was in a worsening financial crisis. Two of its booksellers, including Malcolm Hopkins, had left in 1988, and they were not replaced. The shop was chronically short of money and was only still trading in 1990 with the help of loans from Peacemeal and Peace News Trustees.[10] Their operations gradually contracted as they withdrew from both their Kingsway College branch and wholesale distribution, both of which had become unprofitable. They rented part of the basement to Porcupine Books, a separate second-hand bookshop run by Sandy Donaldson and Andrew Burgin, who had previously worked at Housmans.

Bookshop worker Nigel Kemp explained the pressure the financial situation put on him and the other staff:

A big problem throughout, and I was doing the bookkeeping, was the shortage of cash. It was, what was the next bill we had to pay, and if we paid that bill would we have any money for the next ... we weren't very profitable. If we weren't making any money, we might not have been losing a lot of money but it just wasn't enough, the various activities we did. Apart from stationery and books, we had a bookstall at Kingsway Princeton College. So we had an awful lot of textbooks [to buy] in the term before Christmas, and those had to be paid for. We had the *Peace Diary*, they published maybe 5,000 Peace Diaries, up to 10,000 at one stage. And, the printing bill was several thousand [pounds] ...

---

8   'Railway Threat, Blight and Survival'.
9   Diana Shelley points out that this success was just the beginning of a much longer local struggle, with the Cally Rail Group, which Diana Shelley and Phil Jeffries were both part of, campaigning to mitigate the negative impact of the Channel Tunnel Rail Link. Diana Shelley would stay

involved in this work until 2014.
10  Housmans Board, 'Minutes of Housmans Board Meeting 4 July 1990'.
11  'Minutes of Housmans Board and Staff Meeting 11 December 1991', Housmans Archive, Housmans Minute Book 1990-95.

But the whole time I was there we were struggling to pay the bills. And it's not just finding the money to pay the bills; it's just the strain of it, the strain.

The shop was in danger of trading illegally by placing orders for stock they were unable to pay for. They responded by cutting back on staff, not replacing those who left and eventually making one person redundant in 1991. Now there were only two full-time workers, Nigel Kemp and Craig Liddle, attempting to do work that had been done by six full-time staff in 1981. Minutes of a board and staff meeting held in 1991 reported, understatedly: 'that the scheme of working with only two staff was tolerable, but some modification in the system might be desirable.'[11]

Nigel said that by this point selling stationery was not making money anymore, as businesses began to order from catalogues instead of using local shops. He said

this suited the 'activist people in the shop ... who were quite keen to move more into books ... So eventually ... the back part of Housmans became part of the bookshop.' While this might have been a welcome change for many of the staff, the fall in stationery sales meant less income for the shop and in any case there was not enough money available to keep the shelves full of books. Nigel focused on searching for 'remaindered' books which could be bought cheaply and sold for greater profit.

At the beginning of 1992, sales in the bookshop were down £18,000 in the eight months to 31 December 1991, wiping out any savings that had been made by reducing the staff.[12] In August 1992, a special meeting was held to consider the future of Housmans, gathering the bookshop's board, staff and *Peace News* Trustees. Bookshop worker Craig Liddle presented a paper on behalf of the Housmans staff, outlining their difficulties. The recession of the early 1990s was partly to blame for falling sales, but the radical book trade had been diminishing in general for the last five years. Chain bookshops like Dillons and Waterstones were growing, and there were fears that the Net Book Agreement, which meant all shops had to sell books for the same cover price, would end. Other radical bookshops in London and beyond were closing down, including the CND bookshop, Central Books and Collets (both Central Books and Collets were long-running communist bookshops.) While this situation was far from promising for Housmans, they hoped they might pick up some of the trade from the closed shops; there were not many places left to buy left-wing journals, for instance. The blight caused by the (then) ongoing uncertainty around the Channel Tunnel Rail Link resulted, Craig reported, in 'a fairly demoralised area unattractive to visit and too unpredictable to set up long term business in'. Peace News Trustees reminded the bookshop that they were 'historically committed only to carrying *PN* at a financial loss, and that the bookshop was intended at least to break even'. The meeting concluded that there was 'sufficient confidence' in the bookshop for the moment at least 'not to pursue the issue of closing down'.[13]

Just one month after this meeting, Nigel resigned from Housmans after ten years. He reflected in his interview that 'when I left, my biggest relief was that I didn't have to any longer be the person who was between the people who we owed money to and the bank.' Sandy had already left Peacemeal by this point, also 'feeling a bit burned out'. Together, they set up a second-hand bookshop, Judd Books, just up the road from Housmans in Bloomsbury, which they continue to run to this day. The bookshop recruited a new worker and continued after Nigel's departure to run the shop with just two members of staff.

On 2 May 1993 the *Independent on Sunday* featured Housmans, and its large supply of left newspapers, in an article about the collapse of communism, describing it as 'the last left-wing bookshop in central London ... in a back room in a grubby shop in a street behind King's Cross station'.[14] Albert Beale wrote to the paper to correct the article. He said Housmans did not 'specialise' in 'far left' papers, it was mainly committed to the 'peace movement' and therefore tried to 'facilitate the free discussion of as wide a range of radical and "alternative" ideas as possible'. He hit back at the description of Housmans as 'grubby' by pointing out that the whole area had been blighted by the King's Cross Railway Lands scheme: 'thankfully the local community's struggle ... seems on the verge of victory — otherwise you would soon have to report that there was no remaining central London outlet for the full range of radical literature, grubby or otherwise'.[15]

In the summer of 1994 Craig Liddle was the only full-time member of staff remaining in the bookshop, which was continuing to operate at a loss. He reported to the board that 'with regard to the state of the market for Housmans specialist books, the peace area was dead, the green area was dying, and the only growth area

12   Housmans Board, 'Minutes of Housmans Board and Staff Meeting 29 January 1992', 1992, Housmans Archive, Housmans Minute Book 1990–95.

13   Peace News Trustees, 'Minutes of a Joint Meeting of Peace News Trustees Board and Housmans Bookshop Board and Staff', 1992, Housmans Archive, Housmans Minute Book 1990–95.

14   Alex Renton, 'Communists Collapse, but Reds Stay on Their Marx till the Revolution Comes', Independent on Sunday, 2 May 1983, p. 10.

15   Albert Beale, 'Letter from Housmans to *Independent on Sunday*', 5 May 1993, Housmans Archive, Housmans Minute Book 1990–95.

was gay books.'[16] The board were exploring the possibility of another bookseller buying Housmans, although the bookshop seemed unlikely to be worth much money. At Housmans Annual General Meeting on 9 November 1994, it was noted that the Federation of Radical Booksellers was now defunct.[17]

Meanwhile, Housmans' financial worries were compounded by a series of libel cases brought against the bookshop by right-wing activists, Alexander Baron and Mark Taha, for stocking the anti-fascist magazine, *Searchlight*. They issued over twenty libel writs against organisations and individuals involved in printing, distributing and stocking *Searchlight* (but not against the authors, editors or publishers).[18] They included bookshops like Housmans, Centerprise and Bookmarks in the legal actions even though all they had done was sell the magazine.

In 1995 Housmans settled one case with Baron by paying him £3,200 and issuing a formal apology.[19] However, this was just one of the cases Baron bought: Housmans and Bookmarks refused to settle any others. They set up a Bookshop Libel Fund to attempt to raise the money they needed to fight their case. Around the same time, Albert Beale drafted two amendments to a new Defamation Bill with the support of two MPs, Jeremy Corbyn and Peter Bottomley, hoping to protect 'innocent bystanders' like shops from libel claims.

Albert's amendments did not make it into law, but he felt drafting them had raised awareness of the issue. In 2002, Housmans and Bookmarks lost a case in the High Court, when a jury decided that as the law still stood, the shop could not rely on a defence of 'innocent dissemination', because Baron had sent them a 'gagging letter' before the legal action. However, Baron was only awarded £14 in damages and was ordered to pay Housmans' legal costs as he had refused to settle out of court when he had been offered a higher sum.[20]

Albert said that Housmans:

nearly went to the wall over it financially, because although we were awarded legal costs the guy in that particular instance had no money and couldn't pay them, so we had a five figure sum to raise in order to stop the shop from having to close down. So that was a bit touch and go, it was rather difficult.

In 1995, as the shop faced legal action and considered selling up, Harry Mister

16    'Minutes of Housmans Board and Staff Meeting 20 July 1994', Housmans Archive, Housmans Minute Book 1990 – 95.

17    'Minutes of Housmans Annual General Meeting 9 November 1994', Housmans Archive, Housmans Minute Book 1990 – 95.

18    'Anti-Fascist Articles Prove Rich Pickings', *Independent*, 1996. <https://www.independent.co.uk/news/antifascist-articles-prove-rich-pickings-1338136.html> [accessed 16 June 2022].

19    'Minutes of Housmans Annual General Meeting 9 November 1994'.

20    'Bookshop Loses Landmark Libel Case', *The Bookseller* <https://www.thebookseller.com/news/2002-bookshop-loses-landmark-libel-case> [accessed 4 August 2022].

gathered support to keep it going. He wrote to the board that he had been busy securing donations and recruiting volunteers to help out in the bookshop. Veteran activist Pat Arrowsmith, who had recently retired from her job at Amnesty, would staff the shop two days a week. He wrote he was aware he might 'seem incurably optimistic' but argued that:

> what Housmans with *Peace News* have been able to contribute in the past to the movement for change can and should be continued. We have much of the experience and assets to do this, rather than opting for a close down or transferring our assets to those who do not share the same commitment.[21]

Against all odds, the shop struggled on.

### McLibel and Undercover Spies

In 1989, London Greenpeace had a sudden influx of new activists, all eager to take on jobs and help out. This seemed lucky, as the group at the time had been struggling to attract new people to their meetings. They would later discover that McDonald's had hired two different private detective agencies to spy on the group. Each company, unaware of the other, sent spies to London Greenpeace meetings and admin sessions at 5 Cally Road. McDonald's later admitted at the McLibel trial that at least seven people infiltrated London Greenpeace between October 1989 and Spring 1991 and that they had stolen letters and obtained confidential information about the group and those involved. At times, there were as many spies present at group meetings as genuine activists.

They were not the only members of the group concealing their true identities. Undercover policeman Bob Lambert (or Bob Robinson, as he called himself then) helped to write the factsheet that was the subject of the libel case, unlike any of the five who'd been served the writs.

Bob Lambert aimed ultimately to infiltrate the Animal Liberation Front, with the help of the credibility he built up by being part of London Greenpeace. He did eventually manage to join an ALF cell, which set off incendiary devices in three branches of Debenhams as a protest against fur.[22] The other two members of the cell were arrested, while Bob Lambert began orchestrating his exit from his

---

21 Harry Mister, 'Response to Peace News Trustees and Housmans Bookshop on the Response to a Selected Mailing on Housmans Future', 28 January 1995, Housmans Archive.

22 Evans and Lewis.

LEFT: War Resisters' International office door, 2020

undercover life. By 1989 he was gone, leaving behind two women with whom he had been in relationships, and a child he had had with one of the women.

One of the group members who raised suspicions of the new people joining the group in 1989 was John Barker (later revealed to be John Dines). John Dines was himself an undercover policeman, who took over from Bob Lambert when he had finally disappeared. Dines became the group's treasurer and engineered a long-term relationship with Helen Steel until he also disappeared in 1992.[23]

In 1990, Helen and Dave's refusal to say sorry marked the beginning of what would become the longest running trial in English legal history. They had no legal aid; it was not available for libel cases. In 1991 they challenged this policy in the European Court of Human Rights, but their claim was denied on the grounds that they seemed to be doing a good job of working on their own defence and were therefore not being denied justice.[24] A young barrister, Keir Starmer, gave them free legal advice behind the scenes, and continued to do so throughout the trial. John Dines heard much of the legal advice they were given.

The McLibel Support Campaign was set up by the group very soon after the writs were served.[25] Paul explained how London Greenpeace members focused their energy on supporting the legal battle and the increasingly global mass leafleting and

23    Evans and Lewis.

24    'McLibel: Story' <https://www.mcspotlight.org/case/trial/story.html> [accessed 22 July 2022].

25    'McLibel Support Campaign' <https://www.mcspotlight.org/campaigns/current/msc.html> [accessed 22 July 2022].

publicity campaign:

> Although I apologised, I was still involved in the campaign, and the meetings used to take place at 5 Caledonian Road, I remember that ... I can't remember exactly when they began. They took over from the London Greenpeace meetings. London Greenpeace just changed into [the] McLibel [Support Campaign] for several years, and we stopped having the public meetings at Endsleigh Street ... instead just had group planning meetings or whatever at 5 Caledonian Road. And then they became McLibel meetings really. That's mostly the thing that got discussed. The rest of what the group did just receded into the background ... it was all about McDonald's and the McLibel case for a few years.

Albert pointed out that, as with previous campaigns like the British Withdrawal from Northern Ireland Campaign:

> It was another case where a political trial, if you like, takes a lot of energy and although it does suck in extra support it also takes over the energy of the original campaign whose people who are on trial.

It is no wonder the trial was all consuming: preparing their own defence, even with expert help, was a mammoth task for Helen and Dave. There were four years of preparation, work and preparatory hearings before the main trial even began in 1994. Helen and Dave needed to prepare their defence and arrange witnesses to support the claims made in the leaflet. The McLibel Support campaign collected £35,000 in donations, mostly small amounts from members of the public, which paid for witnesses' travel costs, court expenses and copying documents.[26] When the trial began, McDonald's hired a barrister to whom they paid £2,000 a day to lead a large legal team, while Helen and Dave defended themselves.

Campaigning against McDonald's intensified during the period of the trial. Their leaflet 'What's Wrong With McDonald's' was given so much publicity because of the trial that an updated version was distributed in millions across the UK, translated into over twenty languages and given out all over the world. It is thought to be one of the most widely distributed leaflets ever.[27] Every year there were mass leaflettings held on 16 October, Worldwide Anti-McDonald's Day. In 1996 campaigners launched the 'McSpotlight' website, then a very new way of sharing information. McSpotlight made it possible to share the leaflets, along with other information about McDonald's and the McLibel trial, globally. It had a million hits in its first month.

26  'McLibel Support Campaign'.
27  In the UK, most of the leaflets were printed by London Greenpeace or by Veggies in Nottingham and given to campaigners to distribute outside their local McDonald's. The McLibel Support Campaign calculated that at least three million were printed between 1992 and 1999.

While the McLibel trial was going on, Paul Gravett had, with some other people, set up a new animal rights group, London Animal Action. They shared the London Greenpeace office at 5 Cally Road, while the incredibly busy coordination work of the McLibel Defence Campaign mostly happened in a group member's home.

Paul remembered:

> For a couple of years the office was also London Animal Action. And at this point, another spy enters this story. Matt Rayner [was] his name, and he was infiltrating London Animal Action, and became treasurer of the group. And, he therefore got access to 5 Caledonian Road, [he had] the key [to the office]. So he would be able to go into the office and look at what was there ... And Matt Rayner also spied on the McLibel campaign as well. There are some photos of him at some of the events, some of the protests outside the Royal Courts of Justice that were held during the trial.

In June 1997, the judge gave his verdict in the McLibel trial, following two and a half years and 314 days in court. He found that many of London Greenpeace's claims in the leaflet were true: McDonald's did use deceptive advertising, exploited children, were cruel to animals, were antipathetic to trade unions and paid low wages. However, he found that they had not provided enough evidence that McDonald's destroyed rainforests, that a diet of their food caused heart disease and cancer or gave customers food poisoning, that they were responsible for contributing to starvation in poorer countries, and that their workers had bad working conditions. The judge ruled that Helen and Dave should pay McDonald's £60,000 damages, which they refused to do.

Albert reflected on the day of the judgement:

> It was wonderful in a way, I mean, such a lovely emotional day when the first trial finished and Dave and Helen came out of the court ... it was the biggest crowd of that sort that I'd ever been in. And Dave and Helen, good anarchists both, had to be protected by the police to get them a couple of hundred yards up the road through the crowds to get them into one of the LSE lecture theatres that had been hired for our press conference after the verdict. And one journalist came into our press conference which was chocka, it was standing room only, and said that McDonald's had had a press conference as well, and he'd poked his head in and there was nobody there! They'd all come to the London Greenpeace press conference.

As Albert said, the trial became widely known as 'the biggest corporate own goal in anybody's memory'. Thanks to the trial and campaign, McDonald's had received bad publicity all over the world. Two days after the judgement over 400,000 leaflets were distributed outside 500 UK branches of McDonald's. Helen and Dave were amongst those giving the leaflets out. The campaign had shown it was possible to stand up to a corporation as large and powerful as McDonald's.

The legal case was not over. Helen and Dave appealed against the original verdict and in 1999 the Court of Appeal overturned part of the judgement, finding further key points in their favour and reducing the damages they owed. In 1998, Helen and Dave sued the Metropolitan Police for giving their personal information to McDonald's spies and were paid £10,000 damages plus costs by the police to avoid a trial. Then, in September 2000, they lodged a case with the European Court of Human Rights (ECHR) against the British Government, arguing that the case had breached their rights to a fair trial and to freedom of expression. On 15 February 2005, the ECHR ruled in their favour, mainly because it had not been possible to receive legal aid to defend themselves against the charge of libel.

Albert reflected that in the 1990s, 5 Cally Road was involved in three libel cases, 'one after another', mirroring the criminal trials that had absorbed so much energy and time in the 1970s. These were McLibel, the series of libel writs faced by Housmans between 1996 and 2002 and another case brought against *Peace News* and others by a company that organised arms fairs. By successfully fighting back in the courts and beyond, London Greenpeace had helped reduce the threat libel claims posed to any campaign or organisation seeking to criticise companies and corporations.

The efforts of London Greenpeace members, and in particular Helen Steel, in tracking down and unmasking the undercover policemen that infiltrated their group and their lives helped expose the public scandal of undercover policing. It has emerged that these secret units had infiltrated or targeted over 1,000 left-wing and progressive groups since the late 1960s. This controversy led to the Undercover Policing Public Inquiry, which was announced by then Home Secretary Theresa May in 2015. At the time of writing, the Inquiry is considering fifty-four years of undercover policing, with 247 core participants, including members of London Greenpeace, London Animal Action and the McLibel Support Campaign.[28]

In 2017 a blue plaque was put up on 5 Cally Road by the Campaign Opposing Police Surveillance. It reads 'Peace, Environmental and Animal Rights Campaigns meeting here were spied on by undercover police officers from the Special Demonstration Squad (established 1968), and other units.'

28   'About', *Undercover Policing Inquiry* <https://www.ucpi.org. uk/about-the-inquiry/> [accessed 4 August 2022].

# CHAPTER 8

# SENSE OF PERMANENCE

In 1993 Switchboard moved out of 5 Cally Road to their own building, less than a mile away, and *Peace News* moved back in. Increasingly used by more anti-militarist groups, the building felt like a 'peace centre' again and became an important base for the anti-war movement in the early 2000s.

A new plan to redevelop the area threatened, again, to demolish 5 Cally Road. Once this threat was resolved the bookshop and building began to recover and revive.

### Peace House

With three rooms in the building having opened up after Switchboard left 5 Cally Road, *Peace News* returned after their twenty-year absence. They brought with them War Resisters' International (WRI), who opened their London office in the building. The return of *Peace News* was celebrated as a long-awaited homecoming, while having WRI also based in the building reaffirmed its anti-militarist character.

*Peace News* was emerging from a difficult period when it returned to Cally Road. From 1987 to 1989, it had ceased publication for the first time since it began in 1936. After this break it relaunched and from 1990 joined forces with WRI. It was then published monthly with WRI's support until 1999, when it was published four times a year. An editor was appointed as the paper was no longer run collectively after the relaunch.

Housmans window display

The paper had an international focus at this time, but from 1999 to 2004 was complemented by a sister publication, *Nonviolent Action*, which provided a monthly round-up of grassroots activism around peace, environmental and social justice issues in the UK.

WRI is a global network of pacifists and anti-militarists that was founded in 1921. For a period in the late 1960s and early 1970s, they rented an office next door to 5 Cally Road at number 3, but they had never been based inside the building before. After moving their London office to 5 Cally Road in 1994 they stayed in the building until 2023.

In 1998, Roberta Bacic arrived at 5 Cally Road, having travelled from Chile to work at WRI. She applied for the role having seen the job advertised in *Peace News*. Roberta grew up in Chile and became interested in politics as a teenager. As a young woman she was deeply 'engaged' with the socialist government of Salvador Allende. After Allende's democratically-elected government was overthrown by a CIA-backed coup in 1973, Roberta, like many in Chile, had friends and classmates who disappeared during the dictatorship.

She said:

> I think experience of this kind of life allowed me for the rest of my life to engage in nonviolent action, and actions more for peace, and not to be anti-things but to be pro-things. So that brought me then, many many years later, to War Resisters'.

Roberta described her first impressions of 5 Cally Road:

> I arrived to London in February, on a cold day, and my colleague from War Resisters' … went to pick me up, and brought me to their office. So we entered these little stairs, and I was immediately attracted by the bookshop, and the idea that we would be in a community with many other people … You can read it but it's not the same as to experience it, that we were going to be connected to all those groups, and that *Peace News*, War Resisters' and Housmans Bookshop were all going to be part of a community. So we did many things together, and we spent a lot of time in the office. Nobody worked from home, so we spent long days and had lunch together. And it always felt very warm and very different to the world outside. So it was like a microclimate for us.

*Peace News* and WRI worked closely together in this period. Ippy D, who edited the paper from 1999 and oversaw its transition to a quarterly magazine, remembered *Peace News*' second-floor office as:

> kind of divided into two spaces, WRI had one half and *Peace News* had the other half. But, in the era of cooperation between *Peace News* and WRI that was instigated in the shift to a quarterly paper … one of the first things we did was to take down the wall between these two parts of the office in a kind of symbolic coming together.

Roberta found a sense of community and camaraderie in the building. Her days were structured around a communal lunch hour, with salad and bread prepared on a rota with her colleagues. Roberta was joined in London by her granddaughter, Eva Gonzalez, who arrived when she was five years old. Eva, she says, 'grew up in the building, really'.

Eva remembered helping out with mailouts:

Deliveries [of *Peace News*] had to be made, so we would stuff the envelopes and lick the stamps and sometimes get the dog to lick the stamps, and stick the stamp on the envelope.

She would entertain herself while her grandmother answered emails in the office, playing house on her own under one of the tables. She also became the bookshop's youngest worker:

First it was just organising the bookshelves and making sure all the stationery was full of everything they needed and putting price tags on things. There was a price tag gun thing. Yeah, that was fun. You have to get the right number, and you'd stick it on everything. After that, I was introduced to the till ... And, I remember once insisting that we start charging for plastic bags ... this was before the whole 5p per bag. I think I was charging 20p.

Roberta said:

For me, the building had a very distinctive mark that, it was [both] the place we went to work, and the way we wanted to live. So it was to live in the practice what we had as an idea. We were modest in what we had, we had the culture of sharing, and we had also quite a bit of fun.

Eva Gonzalez helping in the War Resisters' International meeting room

I remember we were involved in not paying the tax that goes to the military. So, we did it for many years, and we had a court case, and we were quite adamant to pursue it as far as we could. And eventually it came to a deadlock, that we had to pay that money to the taxman, because we couldn't continue with the case. But we had promoted it, and we had made it very visible, and we had got lots of support. So, we had every month put the money that we should have paid for that in a little tin. When they came to collect, we had lots of fun, because one of my colleagues prepared a rocket, and we stuck the notes of £5 and £10 on the rocket and gave the man who came to collect the rocket, and a bag with coins. Because we were not willing to draw a cheque saying 'taxman'. We had left the money aside. So it was really a fascinating experience to come [to] agreement, what we were going to do, how we were going to implement, and also think, what do we do if they don't accept it, and start to think what the solutions were. So there was a full year of discussing the strategy at lunchtime on how to continue, and every time we had to go to court we shared it with our friends, and sometimes we stopped at the bookshop and they asked, 'How did it go?' ...

We didn't have to think we have to hide everything in our office, and we have to lock it. We were very open about our actions, we felt safe and at home in the building.

Ippy D grew up in the 1970s, in the northwest of England and went to Greenham Common for the first time when she was fourteen, which was 'a rocket to another planet really'. In the mid-1990s she began writing occasional pieces for *Peace News*. At the time she was involved in grassroots humanitarian aid projects for people affected by war in the former Yugoslavia. She said, 'we had been reading *Peace News*, in an interested fashion, I mean it was our paper.'

In 1999, she was 'happily surprised,' to be appointed editor of *Peace News*, 'given that my main qualifications really related to activism and campaigning'. The early phase of her editorship she described as 'learning on the most steep upward curve I've probably experienced in my life'.

While Ippy was editor, the US and Britain went to war, first in Afghanistan and then in Iraq. She remembered how *Peace News* related to the wider anti-war movement by promoting civil disobedience and direct action:

Peace News tried, I think, very hard to be reflective of and supportive of the international anti-war movement ... And I think, *Peace News* pushed very much for a form of anti-war resistance that went far beyond signing a petition, going on a big demo, but actually trying to get in the way of the war machine, and a form of non-cooperation and direct resistance. And in support very much of other people around the world trying to do the same sort of thing. It was an incredibly busy time for us, both for the paper and also personally in our organising.

Voices in the Wilderness UK moved into office space in 5 Cally Road from 2002. The first Voices in the Wilderness was a group based in the USA that opposed the sanctions imposed on Iraq after the first Gulf War (1990—91) by taking supplies, especially medicines, into Iraq. One of the people who joined these delegations was Milan Rai, now co-editor of *Peace News*. After he returned to the UK he set up Voices in the Wilderness UK. Another member of Voices, Gabriel Carlye, who now works for *Peace News*, described the anti-war activism he was involved with in the run-up to war:

> There was this ramp-up to the invasion of Iraq ... So, there were lots of other groups doing lots of other things, and Stop the War of course famously organises this massive demonstration on 15 February 2003. But we were involved with the other end of it, which was the more direct action side of stuff. So I think it's true that Voices organised the largest single action, nonviolent civil disobedience [action] to what was then the looming invasion of Iraq ... in January 2003. It was just a matter of weeks before the actual invasion took place ... we organised a whole bunch of people to go and blockade Britain's military nerve centre, which is in Northwood, north-west London.

Gabriel explained that 5 Cally Road was used for legal support for this action and was also where campaign newsletters and mail outs were prepared:

> I personally remember being involved in all-night mailings, where we'd have twenty people come and spread out throughout the building at 5 Caledonian Road, to stuff 6,000 envelopes so that we could send out these thousands of newsletters and pamphlets to people all across the country who had signed something ... called the Pledge of Resistance, which was a pledge which thousands of people across the country had signed to take part in nonviolent direct action in the run-up to the invasion of Iraq. So Caledonian Road and *Peace News* were very central to all of this stuff that happened.

On 15 February 2003, just before war was declared on Iraq, demonstrations were held across the world. The march in London was perhaps the biggest the capital has ever seen, with the BBC estimating a million marchers.[1]

> Ippy remembered:
> We wanted to organise something a bit more for after [the march] ... and we also wanted to disseminate a lot of alternative information, to try to incite other people to take their resistance to the bases for example, and do things like stop planes taking off, or stop bombs being loaded, or these kind of things. So, much more direct interventions. And so, out of [5 Cally Road] came a little newspaper specifically for this event, which lots of

---

1    '"Million" March against Iraq War', 16 February 2003
     <http://news.bbc.co.uk/1/hi/uk/2765041.stm> [accessed
     2 August 2022].

different people contributed to ... And we distributed 30,000 that day. And, about 3,000
people stopped at the end of the demo and took part in various acts of civil
disobedience and resistance around London afterwards. And that was organised directly
out of Cally Road.

**Gabriel reflected on the importance of 5 Cally Road at the time:**

I think, for that particular period in 2002 to 2003 especially, it was absolutely essential
that we have some sort of toehold in London. There was no way in hell we would ever
have been able to rent anywhere else on real market rents. But of course, that's the
beauty of the Peace House, is that it doesn't have to charge anything like what anybody
else would have to charge. It's there [for] people who were doing stuff. And so, it was
absolutely crucial for that flurry of activism that happened then.

**The purpose of *Peace News*, as Ippy saw it, was:**

to present a plethora of alternative viewpoints, and to look at power relationships. To
challenge authoritarian structures ... One of the amazing things about *Peace News* is that
it's something where there has been space, historically, for the incoming editors to mould
it to some degree to their own vision, and to reflect their own ideas, and the ideas and
experiences of the groups and networks and so on that those people have been
connected [to] over time.

**Ippy describes the particular perspective she brought as that of 'a feminist, animal-
loving, green, anarchist libertarian' anti-militarist, which she describes as 'a bit of the
spirit of Greenham'.**

I mean to some degree those things are threads that have been running through the
paper for much of its life. But, not entirely, also it's had a very strong association with
conscientious objection, and specific kinds of movements which have been quite
gendered in a different way perhaps, or perhaps not all the gendered kind of experiences
relating to [those movements] were explored in quite the same way, in maybe the forties
and fifties, looking really back into its history. I was the first sole female editor of *Peace
News* in its history; in fact I think I'm still the only [one].

**By 2007, Ippy was ready to move on. Editing *Peace News* was:**

One of the most demanding things I have probably done ... I was quite tired, and, I think,
especially having tried to first take on *Peace News* as it transitioned to a quarterly
magazine ... and then navigating it out of that, and back to a monthly newspaper, after the
Iraq War. And having got through the period of the Iraq War: well Afghanistan first ... and
all our own kind of personal organising, I was absolutely burnt [out].

## Regent's Quarter

Although the King's Cross Railway Lands Bill had been successfully fought off in 1994, the area remained blighted by proposed developments for at least the next decade. Albert describes what the area was like at the time:

There was an era around the turn of the century, when you could walk around from King's Cross station to number five here and probably apart from one odd burger bar, for a lot of the time there'd hardly be anywhere else open. Lots of places were closed down, waiting to be bought and sold or redeveloped or refurbished or whatever it was.

In the early 1970s, when there were plans to site an airport terminal in King's Cross:
the company Stock Conversion (owned by property developer Joe Levy) had bought
up many of the offices and factories in the streets that surrounded 5 Cally Road in the
'Bravington's block', parts of which would later become known as 'Regent's Quarter'.[2]

Diana Shelley explained that in 1983, Stock Conversion came up with a plan
to develop the streets between York Way and Caledonian Road. This would involve
demolishing all the buildings in these blocks, including 5 Cally Road so, Diana Shelley
said, 'it was very clear that … we had to fight it.' Diana wrote her first planning
objection on behalf of the building's Trustees to oppose the plans.
Despite Diana's submission, planning permission was granted for the scheme for the
next fifteen years, although none of the work actually happened. As she says:

> So, what did you get? You got planning blight. You couldn't do this and you couldn't do
> that, and nobody could come in with a better idea because somebody already had a
> fifteen-year stamp on it.

Not long after receiving planning permission, Stock Conversion sold its property to P&O Properties Ltd, along with the permission to develop. Meanwhile, in 1986 the GLC's Historic Building's Division designated a King's Cross Conservation Area, which included the three blocks around 5 Cally Rd.

Much later, in February 2000, P&O submitted a new planning application to develop the area. Its plans included a large office block and hotel but not much residential property, affordable housing or space for shops, restaurants and other things the local community needed. Their plans would also involve demolishing some of the historic industrial buildings in the quarter, which had been listed as valuable by Islington Council since 1978.[3]

Diana remembered how local people were 'consulted':

We weren't allowed to challenge anything. It was a tick-box exercise, as most planning consultations are. The only time that they become real, usually, is when you've managed to give them a bloody nose. And then they go, 'Oh God. Ooh, these uppity peasants, we'd better pay some mind to them.'

Albert Beale remembered that *Peace News* Trustees were approached at this time with an offer to buy 5 Cally Road:

What they more or less said to the trustees at one stage was that they'd bought the land on both sides of us and the land behind us, we were completely surrounded ... we were the one bit in the middle of what they'd got and they wanted to buy us out.

Albert remembered that he and the other trustees were immediately opposed to selling the building:

Part of the basis of radical nonviolence is that you take on board where you are, so inevitably people around 5 Cally have always been involved in local struggles ... So obviously we were sceptical about this, and indeed some individuals ... on the trustees would have blown a gasket if anybody had said 'Oh, well let's sell out to developers.' And the developers came back and said 'Look, you don't understand, you're in the way of our office tower that we want to build at this end of the block, how much do you want?' To which our response was, 'Well you don't understand, fuck off' ... So from that point of view having the building in the hands of people who were politically committed and had the building for political purposes rather than commercial purposes, was important and I think ... that unwillingness of the trustees to go along with a

---

2   Joe Levy had history in the area. Starting in 1952, he had pushed through the huge 'Euston Centre' development up the road from King's Cross, buying up property along Euston Road as he knew the London County Council had plans to widen the road, and using this as leverage to

ensure he got planning permission for what would be one of the biggest developments in twentieth-century London [see Jerry White, *London in the Twentieth Century* (2001)].

3   Angela Inglis and Nigel Buckner, *King's Cross: A Sense of Place* (Leicester: Matador, 2012).

development scheme of that sort was one of the things which helped to fight off the developers on this block.

Diana and Phil lived locally and were active in their local neighbourhood forum, which campaigned to get P&O to listen to what local people wanted. The campaign was so successful that something totally unexpected happened, as Diana explained:

> P&O sacked the architects, went back to the drawing board, and started off by calling meetings with local activists, 'What do you want?' ... we were taken into the buildings ... And we'd sit down, and we'd talk about them, and they'd say, 'Well what do you want?' And we'd go through what we wanted ... They were dealing with us as if we were proper adult human beings. And of course we *were* proper adult human beings. We recognised they needed to make some money. Fine. They're property developers. But in the meantime, please don't pull down these buildings, please create some social rented houses.

In the end, P&O produced a mixed development, refurbishing many of the old buildings and building some new ones which were sensitively mixed in with the old. In 2006 they won a prize from the Islington Society for the best architecture produced that year. There was no need to compulsorily purchase 5 Cally Road and other surrounding buildings. Next door to 5 Cally, at number 7, you can walk through an arch onto a cobbled street to the renovated 'quarter.' Small businesses, including Housmans, and residential buildings on the southern part of Caledonian Road have survived.

### Saving the Shop

While the future of the area was in jeopardy, with many of the surrounding shopfronts boarded up, Housmans had somehow clung on.

In 2007 new staff took over, including Malcolm Hopkins who had worked in the shop in the 1980s. Nik Górecki, a new member of staff, started at the same time. They were joined by Mo Moseley who had worked at the shop on and off since the mid-1980s. Nik described the state of the shop when he started work:

> In 2007 the shop was in a terrible state. There's no way of airbrushing that. The carpet was manky and a good proportion of the shop was filled with dust-covered stationery that had been left over from the era of Harry Mister. The bookshelves were quite understocked. Because the shop was in such deep financial trouble it often meant there wasn't the money to buy new stock. The shop was on 'stop', as it's called, with lots of distributors, and so was spiralling into decline. As I remember it, as you came into the

shop, on the right-hand side, the books were just generic fiction. I guess that in desperation at some point it was decided to stock general fiction as a way to try and make some money, but of course this was diluting the political remit of the shop. It was in a really bad way, but despite that my impression of it was love at first sight. Even then it had something about it that was wonderful. But it definitely felt like it was dying.

Ippy remembered the bookshop as being 'quite tired' and in a 'transitioning phase' in the early 2000s when she worked in the building. 'It felt like it had this dual weight, if you like, of quite trad gay male sort of literature, and then this quite trad, leftist ... quite male literature.' Eva remembered the whole building as run down around the same time:

> It always needed money. The carpets were always very worn and dusty. The hoover was way too old and broke all the time. The sink leaked, a little. The photocopier was broken half the time. I mean the lights worked, but they could have used some help. The building as a whole needed a little bit of love.

In 2000 Ian Dixon reconnected with the building. Ian had been one of the young volunteers who had originally fixed up 5 Cally Road when it first opened. A founder member of the Pacifist Youth Action Group, he later went to prison as one of the 'Wethersfield Six' (see Chapter 1). Ian went to a memorial for Pat Pottle, who had also been in the Committee of 100, and met old friends who were still involved with 5 Cally Road.[4] They persuaded him to think about joining Peace News Trustees, which needed more people involved.

After his time in the Committee of 100, Ian had joined housing campaigns in North Kensington encouraging cooperative housing, campaigned for more council housing and been part of the squatters movement. He then worked for housing associations for the next thirty years, so he had experience of housing and property management.

Ian described what he found when he visited 5 Cally Road for the first time in years:

> The building was sliding into a slough, everyone doing what they had been doing for the last 20 years: no new initiatives, the building was falling into disrepair. And I made a decision, I thought, my background in property is probably the best thing they need at this moment. So I started organising repairs into the building, even later on extending the building ... so we'd have more space for people to rent.

4   Pat Pottle was a founding member of the Committee of
100. He had been imprisoned with Ian, Michael Randle and
others in the early 1960s, and later, with Michael Randle,
helped the Soviet spy George Blake to escape from prison.

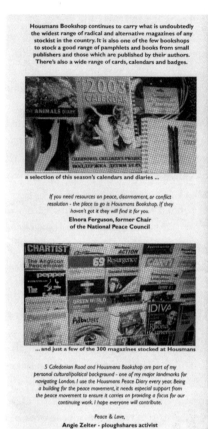

As King's Cross began to emerge from the years of planning blight and work started on redeveloping the Railway Lands behind the stations, there was some money available from the King's Cross Regeneration Fund to fix up the shopfront and building. The trustees needed to raise money to contribute to the cost of the works and so they made a 'once in a lifetime' appeal to their supporters for contributions to renovate the bookshop and building. A leaflet was produced showcasing the work of the building and bookshop and appealing for donations. It included messages of support from prominent peace activists like Bruce Kent, the local MP Chris Smith, and well-known people who had used the building over the years, like Helen Steel and Dave Morris.[5]

5    Peace News Trustees, 'Building for Campaigning',
     Bishopsgate Institute, 5 Cally Road archive.

Leaflet produced as part of the 'Housmans Relaunch Appeal' to refurbish 5 Caledonian Road

*Housmans has provided a radical and excellent service for many years.
It thoroughly deserves not only to survive but to thrive into the future.
I would urge strong support for this appeal.*

**Chris Smith - MP for Islington South & Finsbury,
the Housmans constituency**

*I'm delighted to learn that 5 Caledonian Road, home from home for
so many good and peaceful causes over the years, is due for a facelift.
I won't be the only one to dig deep to help make sure that Number 5
remains presentable and useful for a long time to come.*

**Bruce Kent**

*"For many years London Greenpeace has been able to use 5 Cally Road
for meetings, for its address, and for some of the time for an office.
The premises, and the shop below, have been a friendly and accessible
lifeline for a whole range of activities. Our meetings there were infiltrated
by agents of McDonald's and the premises became the base for the
hugely successful McLibel Support Campaign. We send our solidarity
and support to the building renewal project."*

**Helen Steel and Dave Morris - the McLibel Two**

### how you can help

This is not another annual appeal; this is a once (well, OK, maybe twice)
in a lifetime appeal, to re-launch 5 Caledonian Road as a valuable -
and viable - resource for the radical movement of the 21st century.
Even before this appeal was publicly launched, several people had offered
£1,000 each to start us off.

We know that if we are to reach our targets, then much of the money
will have to come from a number of major donations. But please don't let
that put any of you off - we need all the help we can get, and a successful
revamp at 5 Caledonian Road will work best with the goodwill, thoughts,
and help of lots of people, given in their own way and according to their
own abilities and resources.

**We warmly welcome any donation of any size.** Of course we
would also welcome any offers of practical help in promoting the shop
and other areas of our work here, and donations of relevant books for
our secondhand books section. If you could spare a significant sum, but
only as a loan for a few years, not a donation, we would be only too
happy to accept! Please contact us if you think you can help.

We would also welcome suggestions of other people to whom we
should send this appeal. You could circulate copies of this appeal yourself
of course, just contact us for extra copies.

We will soon need to be able to pay for our share of the work which
is partly funded by the building regeneration project - so at least some of
our need is urgent. But, in order to make the most of this opportunity,
we need to undertake other improvements, and be able to underwrite
improved levels of staffing, equipping and promotion of the shop as soon
as possible thereafter.

So we need to get a significant proportion of our target figure
quite soon - certainly within a few months. That doesn't mean that
if we don't get the full amount straight away then what we do get will
be wasted: some of the developments can be phased. But for the best
results, we need to go for the 'Big Bang' approach.

We encourage you to support this Housmans Appeal, to
maintain and develop this valuable, broad-based, non-sectarian
supplier of radical literature in central London.

Peace News Trustees (Housmans Relaunch Appeal)
5 Caledonian Road, London N1 9DY
020 8673 0670
iandixon@btinternet.com

### current challenges

Since the 1980s, much of the immediate area has been derelict, with
half the offices, shops and cafes empty. Property companies have
bought up most of the area - at one time with plans (now defeated)
to raze several blocks and build an 'office city' on the site. For years
the area was blighted by road and rail plans now abandoned. Inevitably
this affected the ability to attract customers, and passing trade was
limited. With the immediate area now, finally, being refurbished, this is
exactly the right time for Housmans to invest in its future.

There have been the changes in the book trade, such as the end of the
Net Book Agreement, and the special problems of radical bookshops
who have seen some of their most profitable areas creamed off by the
big chains, but we are convinced that a specialist shop like Housmans,
concentrating on its uniqueness, can thrive.

The investment made in the building in the 1950s has served us well
but every spare penny went into supporting the work - frequently
unprofitable (in financial terms) - being done in the building. **Now
the shop and the building need a fresh injection of capital to
revitalise them so that they can continue to provide a service
for current and future generations of campaigners.**

**Especially crucial is the need for the shop to be refurbished.**
Housmans is the main public face of the building, and the part which
serves the widest range of people. It needs to attract passing trade for
its 'bread and butter' income as well as providing an efficient service for
its specialist customers, in person and by mail order, from all over the
world. And, of course, if the shop thrives, it helps to provide a secure
economic basis for the rest of the building.

Housmans Bookshop and the services and facilities offered
by 5 Caledonian Road have a long and varied history. The
recent past has been difficult, but we are convinced that
there is a vibrant future ahead, where 5 Caledonian Road and
Housmans Bookshop will play a vital part in campaigning for
peace and social change.

After 2007, the area slowly revitalised. Footfall improved and the future of the
bookshop began to look brighter. Nik reflected on how Malcolm Hopkins especially
helped to turn the bookshop around:

> One of the things that he really brought to the shop was a lifetime of bookselling
> experience, and a very cold, hard approach to the finances ... He really got to grips with
> that and saved the shop. There's no two ways about it. I did a lot more of the decorative
> work to get the shop looking the part, but when it came to making the tough decisions
> in the background, I think Malcolm absolutely saved the shop.

Nik remembered the 'reforms' they made to turn the shop around:

> One of those was slashing our wages to minimum wage, and another was to start asking
> volunteers to come and help run the shop. With staffing levels of barely one person a day,
> there's only so much you can do; serving customers is a job in itself so you could never

catch up with the backlog of other things that needed to be done. So, we started inviting volunteers, and thankfully we had many great volunteers over the years, whose contribution is huge.

The shop is now run collectively by a team of four booksellers: Catherine Barter, Cristina Rios, Dee Creative and Nik Górecki.

In the past, the bookshop staff were employed by the Housmans board, who had ultimate decision-making power over the shop. In practice, since Harry Mister's retirement a collective of the shop staff made decisions about how to run the shop day-to-day, but when difficult issues arose there could be conflict with the board. Now the bookshop staff are all directors of the company, which means they can manage the shop cooperatively with the support of non-staff members who also sit on the board. Nik said the shop is now in 'a very good place', it is financially stable and the staff feel empowered:

[Becoming directors] had quite a profound effect. It might be quite a subtle difference, but when you think, I'm a director, and at the end of the year have to sign off on the shop's finances ... you do have a greater sense of responsibility than you might [do] as just an employee.

Bookshelves at Housmans, 2019

In 2015 Housmans fundraised to renovate 'the vaults' in one of the basement rooms. These old coal vaults extend under the pavement at the front of the shop. Glass set into the pavement lets in a little light from above. The new room created space to develop the range of books Housmans carried, as Nik explained:

> We created new fiction, art, poetry and children's book sections, and really expanded the range of the stock, and the space of the shop as well. If you include the vaults and the downstairs second-hand section we have nearly doubled the shopfloor area.
>
> And over the last decade or so we've put a lot of work into refining and renewing the sections. For example, if you go back twelve years there wasn't much of a feminism section. I gather the shop has been primarily run by men throughout its history, and it's only now for the first time that we have a majority female-run shop. And, surprise, surprise, next thing you know, we've got a brilliant feminism section.

Apart from feminism, other areas that have grown in recent years, as bookseller Catherine Barter explained, are black politics, anti-racist politics and queer politics. She saw nonviolence as underpinning what they stocked 'because I think there's a kind of guiding belief that all these liberation politics are ultimately what moves us towards more a more peaceful world'. Catherine described Housmans as aiming to curate a 'broad church bookshop of the left'.

The vaults in the basement of Housmans bookshop, 2020

Nik described their role as curators:

We work hard as a staff to try and pick a great selection of books, some that you will know, and some that you won't, and try [to] cover the whole spectrum of publishing from a radical point of view. I think that curation is something we bring that you can't get from just looking at an online shop ... the picking of the books, and presenting them, updating them, and promoting what's politically relevant at any given time. Importantly, Housmans isn't partisan. Unlike some other radical bookshops we try to cover everything and do it in an open-ended, [broad] church fashion, having competing ideas next to each other on the shelf.

Housmans entices customers in through its doors to attend its book groups (there's a general one as well as a Black Feminist book club, a Queer book club and one for reading Feminist sci-fi) and a programme of regular events, which were held in person before the pandemic began in 2020; book launches, discussions and meetings organised by outside groups. During the pandemic, events began to be held online, allowing people to join from around the world.

Catherine said she enjoys people discovering the bookshop for the first time, as well as talking to customers who have been visiting the shop for decades:

I quite like working somewhere where it feels like we're carrying on a legacy, keeping something safe in a way to pass on hopefully to whoever's going to manage it next, and just having a sense of it being part of a long, continuing, really valuable centre.

Nik pointed out that an advantage of 5 Cally Road and Housmans is 'it's a place where you can launch new projects from'. One such was the Alliance of Radical Booksellers, inspired by the earlier Federation of Radical Booksellers, which now connects radical bookshops around the country. Another was the Bread and Roses Book Prize, which is an annual award given to the best radical book, and the Little Rebels Book Prize, which is awarded to the best radical children's book. Housmans has also been part of organising bookfairs like the London Radical Bookfair and the Anarchist Festival in recent years.

Catherine, who is one of the organisers of the Little Rebels Award described how it was developed by Letterbox Library, an inclusive children's booksellers and is now part of a general move towards inclusivity, diversity and social justice themes in children's publishing. The visibility the prize gives these books helps them reach beyond the world of radical bookshops to reach a wider range of people.

In 2007 Ippy D was succeeded as editor of *Peace News* by Milan Rai and Emily Johns. The paper is now published independently of WRI every two months, both as a paper edition and online. It has an office based at 5 Cally Road, which it shares with Forces Watch and Network for Peace. *Peace News* has five members of staff, who work together as a non-hierarchical working group and are supported by a board of

directors. The staff all work part-time on the paper and spend the rest of their time as campaigners, writers or artists.

Staff member Gabriel Carlyle described the importance of the paper today:

Peace News covers ... the whole spectrum of activism that's taking place in the UK, and beyond the boundaries of the UK as well, but it's not siloed in the way that quite a few of the other publications that still exist [are] ... So it's ... a paper for activists, by activists, covering a whole spectrum of those movements, and with a commitment to nonviolence. And there's nothing else in the UK which ticks all of those boxes....

And the fact that it's still in print [is important] as well. Online, yes, you could stumble across something ... but then you're really relying upon our digital overlords, algorithms, to put that in front of you. Whereas with [a printed paper] you can take it ... to any demonstration that you can physically reach, and you can put it into someone's hand, and you can have a conversation.

Peace News has run several special projects in the last decade aimed at bringing people from different activist movements together. These include the Peace News Summer Camp (2009 — 18), the Rebellious Media Conference (2011), which over 1,000 people attended, and a series of talks and exhibitions that celebrated opposition to the First World War at the time of the war's centenary (2014 — 18). Peace News Press publishes books, including an account of the Seeds of Hope action and trial in 1996, The Hammer Blow: How Ten Women Disarmed a Warplane (2016).

After spending fifteen years as chair of Peace News Trustees, Ian Dixon felt the building was in a good place; 'a few years ago, we got to the stage where we had maximised the space in the building, we had prepared everything, we had actually introduced fire regulations.' At the time of writing, the building is full of small offices spread over four floors. Tenants include War Resisters' International, the Oromo Relief Association, Campaign Against Climate Change, No Sweat and the Federation of Iraqi Refugees. The affordable rent from their offices helps to maintain the building and supports Peace News and Housmans.

During the COVID-19 pandemic many businesses in King's Cross closed, echoing the feeling the area had in the early 2000s when many of the shopfronts were also boarded up. But even in the midst of the uncertainty of the pandemic, Nik reflected, 'It's that sense of permanence that I think is really important ... that no matter what else may be happening, the building is solid and we'll still be here.'

This book has its origins — as has so much else — through a lucky encounter in Housmans bookshop. One morning I met Nik Górecki, who suggested a history project about 5 Caledonian Road, and eventually one happened.

Thank you everyone who contributed their memories, possessions, expertise and time to this book and the wider project it is a part of. It is the culmination of a lot of collective work. Thank you to everyone for your patience. A list of people who contributed to the project is below, apologies to anyone left off in error.

Funding from the National Lottery Heritage Fund made the project (and this book) possible; thank you to National Lottery players for their contributions and the Heritage Fund for their support.

Thank you especially to all those who read and commented on the text.

Thank you to all at Housmans Bookshop, Peace News, Peace News Trustees Ltd (especially Alice Kadel), the 5 Cally Road project's steering group and everyone who has been been part of 5 Cally Road over the years.

Thank you to Anne Beech for proofreading the text with great skill and speed. Any errors that remain are my responsibility alone.

Thank you to Guglielmo Rossi for your creative and thoughtful typesetting and design.

Thank you to all at Bishopsgate Institute, especially Stef Dickers, for allowing us to use some of their incredibly rich archives in this book and for giving the 5 Cally Road archive a home.

Thank you to all the institutions that allowed the use of their archive material: Anna Towlson at the LSE Library; the International Institute of Social History; Tudor Allen at Camden Archives, Alan Dein and Leslie McCartney from King's Cross Voices for letting us use excerpts from Harry Mister's interview; and Switchboard, especially Tash Walker. Special thanks to Julie Parry and the Special Collections and Archives at Bradford University.

Thank you to Catherine Packard, Douglas Cape and John Carroll for allowing the use of their photographs.

Thank you to Susan Hutton and Susan Nicholls for transcription of the interviews.

Thank you to Lucy Allen, and everyone who collaborated on the earlier part of this project, which culminates in the publication of this book.

As always, thank you to Richard Whittell for everything including being willing to edit my writing and for always being honest about how it could be better. Thank you most of all to Leo and Reuben, you are both amazing and I'm sorry for all the time I spent writing this book.

## Interviews with:
Albert Beale, Alexander Donaldson, Ann Feltham, Ann Willis, Bob Overy, Bruce Kent and Valerie Flessati, Catherine Barter and Nik Górecki, Clifford Williams, Dashty Jamal, Diana James, Diana Shelley, Emily Johns, Eva Gonzalez, Gabriel Carlyle, Geoff Hardy, Ian Dixon, Ippy D, Jim Huggon, John Lloyd, Julian Hows, Lesley Mair, Martyn Lowe, Maryam Namazie, Michael Randle, Mike Jackson, Mo Moseley, Nettie Pollard, Nigel Kemp, Paul Gravett, Ramsay Kanaan, Roberta Bacic, Rosie Ilett, Steve Craftman, Stuart Feather, Sue Aubrey, William Hetherington

## Archive donated by:
Alexander Donaldson, Andrew Rigby, Ann Feltham, Ann Willis, Clifford Williams, Dashty Jamal, Dave Morris, Gemma Curtis, Geoff Hardy, Ian Dixon, Lelia Kassir, Lesley Mair, Martyn Lowe, Michael Randle, Mike Jackson, Peace News Trustees Limited, Roberta Bacic.

## Project volunteers:
Agata Cienciala, Alex Mulholland, Anna Thomson, Anoushka Chakrapani, Camden Graves, Christina Radukic, Connie Hatt, Daniel Gayne, Despina Kalogianni, Honor Morris, Joss Harrison, Keir Chauhan, Laura Patari, Laura Toms, Lauryn Grant, Lottie Korn, Lydia Everett, Marie Cabadi, Megan Drabble, Mitra Karanjkar, Naoise Murphy, Reece Evans, Sara Babhemi, Soph Woodruff, Tania Aubeelack, Therese Ahossey, Will Hecker, Xiaoman Huang, Zuza Wolfram.

LEFT TO RIGHT: Housmans 1959, Porcupine Bookshop in the basement of Housmans, police and crowd outside Housmans bookshop

**p. 2** © Daniel Gayne, 5 Cally Road archive, Bishopsgate Institute
**p. 6 left** Courtesy of Rosie Ilett, 5 Cally Road archive, Bishopsgate Institute
**p. 6 right** © Alexander Donaldson, 5 Cally Road archive, Bishopsgate Institute
**p. 9** Courtesy of Clifford Williams, 5 Cally Road archive, Bishopsgate Institute
**p. 14** Images courtesy of Peace News and Michael Randle
**p. 17 top** Courtesy of Peace News Trustees, 5 Cally Road archive, Bishopsgate Institute
**p. 17 bottom** © Derek Brook archive, Bishopsgate Institute
**p. 18** © Derek Brook archive, Bishopsgate Institute
**p. 21 right** © Peace News
**p. 21 left** Courtesy of Ann Willis, 5 Cally Road archive, Bishopsgate Institute
**p. 22 right and left** Courtesy of Peace News Trustees, 5 Cally Road archive, Bishopsgate Institute
**p. 24** Courtesy of Michael Randle, 5 Cally Road archive, Bishopsgate Institute
**p. 27** © Peace News
**p. 31** © Peace News
**p. 32** Images courtesy of Peace News
**p. 37** © Peace News
**p. 38** © Peace News
**p. 41** © Peace News
**p. 48** © Peace News
**p. 49** Courtesy of Bishopsgate Institute
**ARCHIVE SECTION 1**
**p. 50** photographer unknown. Courtesy of Peace News Trustees, 5 Cally Road archive, Bishopsgate Institute
**pp. 50–54** Courtesy of Michael Randle, 5 Cally Road archive, Bishopsgate Institute
**pp. 51–54** © Derek Brook archive, Bishopsgate Institute
**pp. 57–58** Courtesy of Alexander Donaldson, 5 Cally Road archive, Bishopsgate Institute

**pp. 56, 59** © Brian Hart/ Campaign for Homosexual Equality Archive, Bishopsgate Institute
**pp. 59–62** Courtesy of Hall Carpenter Archives, London School of Economics Library
**p. 63** Courtesy of David McLellan archive, Bishopsgate Institute
**p. 64** Images courtesy of London School of Economics, Bishopsgate Institute
**p. 67** Courtesy of LGBTQ+ Archives, Bishopsgate Institute
**p. 68** Courtesy of Hall Carpenter Archives, London School of Economics Library
**p. 73** Courtesy of Hall Carpenter Archives, London School of Economics Library
**p. 74** © LGBTQ+ Archives, Bishopsgate Institute
**p. 76** Images courtesy of Peace News, Campaign Against Arms Trade, 5 Cally Road archive, Bishopsgate Institute
**p. 79** © Campaign Against Arms Trade
**p. 81** © Peace News
**p. 84** Courtesy of the International Institute of Social History, Amsterdam
**p. 87** Images courtesy of Peace News Trustees, 5 Cally Road archive, Bishopsgate Institute.
**p. 89** © NLA/reportdigital.co.uk
**p. 90** © Morning Star Photographic archive, Bishopsgate Institute
**p. 92** Images courtesy of Switchboard archive, Bishopsgate Institute, Robert Workman archive, Bishopsgate Institute.
**p. 95** © Switchboard archive, Bishopsgate Institute
**p. 95** © Robert Workman archive, Bishopsgate Institute
**p. 96** © Switchboard archive, Bishopsgate Institute
**p. 97** © Switchboard archive, Bishopsgate Institute
**p. 98** © Robert Workman archive, Bishopsgate Institute
**p. 99** © Switchboard archive, Bishopsgate Institute

**p. 101 top** © Switchboard archive, Bishopsgate Institute
**p. 101 bottom** © Robert Workman archive, Bishopsgate Institute
**p. 103 right and left** © Robert Workman archive, Bishopsgate Institute
**p. 105** Courtesy of Alexander Donaldson, 5 Cally Road archive, Bishopsgate Institute
**p. 106** Images courtesy of Alexander Donaldson, Clifford Williams and Peace News Trustees
**p. 109** © Pam Isherwood, Format archive, Bishopsgate Institute
**p. 110** © Peace News
**p. 111** © CAAT, 5 Cally Road archive, Bishopsgate Institute
**p. 112** © CAAT, 5 Cally Road archive, Bishopsgate Institute
**p. 113** Courtesy of Peace News Trustees, 5 Cally Road archive, Bishopsgate Institute
**p. 116** Courtesy of Rosie Ilett, 5 Cally Road archive, Bishopsgate Institute
**p. 117** © Alexander Donaldson, 5 Cally Road archive, Bishopsgate Institute
**p. 118** © Alexander Donaldson, 5 Cally Road archive, Bishopsgate Institute
**p. 119 left** Courtesy of Peace News Trustees, 5 Cally Road archive, Bishopsgate Institute
**p. 119 right** Courtesy of Rosie Ilett, 5 Cally Road archive, Bishopsgate Institute
**pp. 120–121** © Alexander Donaldson, 5 Cally Road archive, Bishopsgate Institute
**p. 122** © Alexander Donaldson, 5 Cally Road archive, Bishopsgate Institute
**p. 123** Courtesy of Alexander Donaldson, 5 Cally Road archive, Bishopsgate Institute
**p. 124** © Clifford Williams, 5 Cally Road archive, Bishopsgate Institute
**p. 125** Courtesy of Alexander Donaldson, 5 Cally Road archive, Bishopsgate Institute

p. 128 Courtesy of Peace News Trustees, 5 Cally Road archive, Bishopsgate Institute

**ARCHIVE SECTION 2**

p. 129 © Peace News

p. 130 © CAAT, 5 Cally Road archive, Bishopsgate Institute

p. 131 © Robert Workman archive, Bishopsgate Institute

pp. 132–135 © Switchboard archive, Bishopsgate Institute

pp. 131–134 Courtesy of Mike Jackson, 5 Cally Road archive, Bishopsgate Institute

pp. 135–136 © Robert Workman archive, Bishopsgate Institute

pp. 137–142 Courtesy of Alexander Donaldson, 5 Cally Road archive, Bishopsgate Institute

p. 141 Courtesy of Alexander Donaldson, 5 Cally Road archive, Bishopsgate Institute

p. 144 Images courtesy of Dave Morris, Alexander Donaldson, Peace News Trustees. 5 Cally Road archive, Bishopsgate Institute

p. 147 © Douglas Cape z360.com

p. 148 © John Carroll

p. 149 Courtesy of Dave Morris, 5 Cally Road archive, Bishopsgate Institute

p. 150 Courtesy of Dave Morris, 5 Cally Road archive, Bishopsgate Institute

p. 152 © Catherine Packard

p. 155 © Alexander Donaldson, 5 Cally Road archive, Bishopsgate Institute

p. 156 Courtesy of Peace News Trustees, 5 Cally Road archive, Bishopsgate Institute

p. 160 left © Daniel Gayne, 5 Cally Road archive, Bishopsgate Institute

p. 160 right Photograph by Laura Mitchison © On the Record

p. 164 Images © Sophie Polyuiou, 5 Cally Road archive, Bishopsgate Institute

p. 166 Courtesy of Peace News Trustees, 5 Cally Road archive, Bishopsgate Institute

pp. 168–169 © Roberta Bacic, 5 Cally Road archive, Bishopsgate Institute

p. 173 © Catherine Packard

p. 174 © Catherine Packard

p. 178 © Peace News Trustees, 5 Cally Road archive, Bishopsgate Institute

p. 180 © Sophie Polyuiou, 5 Cally Road archive, Bishopsgate Institute

p. 181 top Photograph by Laura Mitchison © On the Record

p. 181 bottom © Anoushka Chakrapani, 5 Cally Road archive, Bishopsgate Institute

p. 183 © Sophie Polyuiou

p. 186 Images courtesy of Peace News Trustees, Alexander Donaldson, Bishopsgate Institute

First published by Housmans, 2023

Housmans
5 Caledonian Road
London
N1 9DX

《《OnTheRecord

British Library Cataloguing in Publication Data
A CIP catalogue record for this book is available from the British Library

ISBN 9780 85283 285 1

This book was designed, typeset and made into pages in Adobe
InDesign by Guglielmo Rossi, Bandiera, London.
The book was printed and bound by Gomer Press, Wales.

This publication was published with financial support from The
National Lottery Heritage Fund.

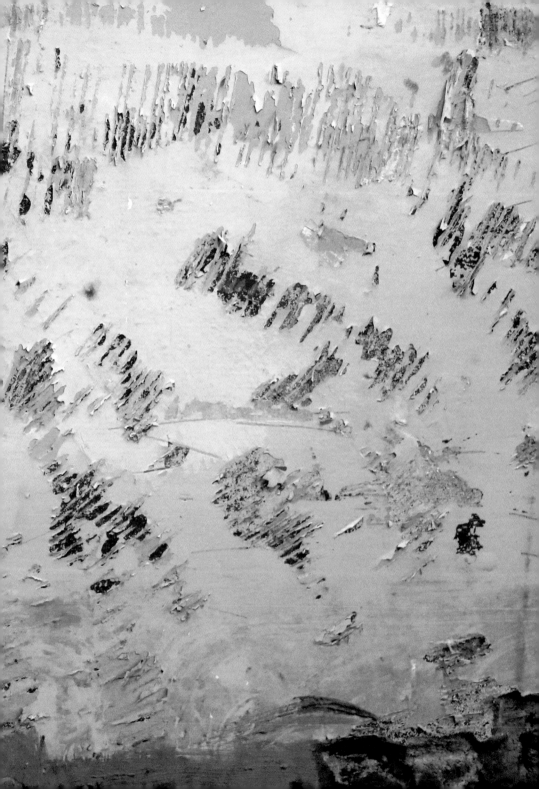